Praise for the yforum website . . .

"A space where readers can safely follow a dialogue on sensitive topics without having to wade through racist attacks, foul language or flame wars."

—The Atlantic Monthly

"One of the most inventive uses of a technology that is too often dismissed as a glorified toy or a gigantic shopping mall."

—The Boston Globe

"Mr. Milano has dared to open the field of debate to the maximum. Finally, the universal impact of the Internet is beginning to be felt."

—Le Monde

"[A] remarkable contribution to cross-cultural understanding."

—The Guardian

"So long as we are mysteries, one to another, we face a perpetuation of ignorance and a feeding of fear. That's why Y? has a profound appeal to me."

—nationally syndicated columnist Leonard Pitts

Acknowledgments

I Can't Believe You Asked That! started with a hunch I had seven years ago that people wanted a safe, civil way to talk about their differences. It wouldn't have been possible without the help of many people.

First and foremost, I want to thank my contributing researchers, who helped me track down expert answers to many of the questions in this book. My "Y? Team," as I like to call them, consisted of Steve Patterson, David Bauer, Dan Scanlan, and John Carter. Thank you all for your creative approaches and dedication.

I'd also like to offer my deep gratitude to the following for their assistance:

Grant McManus, for his love, wisdom, and advice during the good times and the frustrating ones, and for the design of the *Y?* website graphics.

Larry Lane, who provided invaluable editing assistance and guidance for the book that served as the forerunner to *I Can't Believe You Asked That!* titled *Why Do White People Smell Like Wet Dogs When They Come Out of the Rain? And Other Questions Worth a Smack on the Head from Mom.*

Margret McBride, Renee Vincent, and everyone at Margret

McBride Literary Agency, and John Duff at Perigee Books, for their guidance and work in helping put the Y? project before a new and larger audience.

Susan Scott, for forcing me not to give up and for introducing me to McBride Literary.

Drew Dials, who provided endless hours of database computer programming for the Y? website at a very reasonable (unheard of) price.

Pat and Pete Duerfeldt and Jack and Carol Dycus, for providing their moral support and their advice during the question selection phase of *I Can't Believe You Asked That!*

Leonard Pitts, Josh Silverman, Joy Mills, Joe Adams, and Nicole McGill, for believing in Y?

The Florida Times-Union, for allowing me to embark independently on a project that has not been without its controversy.

My wife and children and my parents and brothers, for their encouragement and love as I undertook this unpredictable and often stressful project.

Finally, my website users, who provided so many eye-opening submissions for this project—and the evidence that people do, in fact, want to ask the questions and hear the answers.

Contents

I Can't Believe You Asked THAT!

Introduction

Zandria and I were on a plane headed to a newspaper conference in Washington, D.C. I had hired her, a black female, to run a job bank that I'd set up to help newspapers nationwide stir a little more color into their ranks.

We'd gotten to know each other well enough that, for whatever reason—probably because I have an obsessive desire to prove to myself I can be likable no matter what comes out of my mouth—I decided on that fall day several years ago to ask her one of *those* questions.

You know the kind I'm talking about. The really hairy questions you wish you could serve up to someone who's so different from you they might as well be from another planet, or at least a regular on *The Jerry Springer Show.*

What the heck, I thought. *Fire away.*

"So Zandria, I'm wondering, when I see these black hosts on urban talk shows, how come they always seem to be acting almost too black? I mean, everything's, you know, 'Yo, wassup' and 'So-and-so's inna house' and 'He da bomb.' What's that all about?"

I waited. I mean, at least I hadn't asked her something about black women's bottoms.

Finally she smiled.

"Phil, you think me and my friends are thinking about whether those guys are acting black? That's just who we are when we're together. When you watch Jay Leno, do you think about whether he's acting white? Everybody talks and acts differently in different places. I may talk differently when I'm partying than when I'm in the office, but I'm not acting black."

Whoa. I felt like I should fire up the ol' American melting pot and jump in when it started a nice rolling boil. But at least her serving tray was not in the upright and locked position deep within my scrawny white buttocks.

What Zandria did that day, with her patience and humor, was help nurture the seed of an idea I'd been turning over in my head for some time: What if people had a nonlethal way of asking those mightily embarrassing questions they've always wanted to ask but never do for fear of being called out as a racist, a homophobe, or worse?

It's not as if the mainstream media feature people in no-holds-barred discussions about squirmy cross-cultural topics. Far from it. In fact, I've talked with more than one newspaper editor who thinks that the public would be offended by it at best and horrified at worst.

Instead, rather than try to clue us in about our differences, the media focus on the peculiar things that happen precisely because of our general cluelessness about one another. Take a quick look at any paper on any given day. You're more than likely to see stories like these, all of which happened over a recent span of just several weeks:

- Target Stores apologizes and pulls its line of shorts and baseball caps emblazoned with "EIGHT EIGHT," "EIGHTY EIGHT," and "88"—saying its buyers didn't realize the phrases were neo-Nazi hate symbols meaning "Heil Hitler."

- After complaints from Hispanic groups, the owner of a Massachusetts-based costume maker defends his company's "Vato Loco" Halloween mask—a brown-skinned caricature of a gang member with tattoos and a bandanna—saying it must be okay because it is made by Mexican factory workers. He later threatens to adorn the cover of his customer catalog with a picture of "Vato Loco," which in English roughly translates to "crazy, street-tough guy."

- A Warner Bros. spokeswoman defends the film company's record on social issues but says an ending scene in *Harry Potter and the Chamber of Secrets* depicting a straitjacketed character won't be edited out, despite complaints from advocates for the mentally *ill* who decry it as "a cruel parody."

- A large software developer announces it will cut several scenes from a hot-selling video game after being deluged with complaints that it encourages violence against Sikhs. The initial version of *Hitman 2—Silent Assassin* by United Kingdom–based Eidos Interactive invites players to come along on "20 missions to assassinate corrupt" leaders. In one, players enter the Golden Temple—the Sikhs' holiest shrine—to kill bearded Sikh "terrorists" in turbans.

- Wal-Mart finds itself facing the prospect of the largest civil rights class-action suit in history after female workers charge the behemoth retailer with systematic sex discrimination. Among the allegations: A female employee seeking a promotion was told it was a man's world and that men controlled Wal-Mart, while another, questioning why better jobs were given to men less qualified than her, was told by a store manager that she "needed to blow the cobwebs off" her makeup and "doll up."

- Members of a white fraternity at Oklahoma University apologize after photos from their "Come as You Are Bizarre" party are posted on the Internet, including one of a member in black-face standing between two frat brothers—one wearing a Klan costume and the other in overalls and a Confederate flag bandanna. A mock noose dangles above the black-faced member's head.

And on and on.

Such "Moronic Miscue of the Week" coverage doesn't come close to shedding real light on the growing cultural divide in the United States. It provides a random spotlight when a full complement of relentless searchlights is required. When national studies show that more than 70 percent of Americans feel racial groups aren't getting along well with each other, worry that things are only going to get worse, and think racial and religious tension is a serious problem, a bolder approach to cultural education is desperately needed—one that finally rips off the blinders of propriety and the muzzles of decorum that have stanched the flow of frank talk about our differences for decades.

That's where Y? The National Forum on People's Differences comes in. During the months after my talk with Zandria, I slowly began to realize that the perfect place for people to start fearlessly discussing their differences was that warm, fuzzy bastion of global anonymity called cyberspace. I starting tinkering with the idea of a cross-cultural Internet forum with no cause or agenda attached to it other than to get people talking. After a while, contemplating my navel gradually gave way to building web pages. When I was ready, I registered with the big search engines and sent out e-mails to all my friends, family, and people I knew in the newspaper business, telling them what I was doing: I was going to moderate a national dialogue on sensitive cultural differences, and I wanted them to help kick off things with a question or answer.

I stood at the ready. Soon I started getting some hits. And postings. A question here, an answer there. Nothing earth-shaking, but a start.

And reaction? You want reaction?

"This is another pathetic liberal project."

"Queers aren't getting their say."

"You're doing the same thing Adolf Hitler did to the Jews in Nazi Germany."

"Y? sucks! It's nothing more than dumb-ass white people asking stupid questions about other people (mostly blacks)."

"This site is way too politically correct."

"I can't believe how much politically incorrect content you allow."

"Why do minorities get to post the tough questions and answers, but not whites?"

"Why is it okay for white males to run scams on the Internet?"

So much for feedback.

Thankfully, those weren't the only reactions. A break came when Leonard Pitts, an author and nationally syndicated columnist with *The Miami Herald,* heard about Y? and scribed, for lack of a better description, the greatest newspaper column ever written, the topic of which happened to be my project and the fact that it was pretty damn cool. I was stunned by the response. Dozens of newspaper reviews and TV and radio talk show interviews followed. It was all I could do to get to the hundreds of posts coming in from all over the world, working in the milky hours of the morning before my wife and kids got up, laughing at the hilarity of some of the postings, even getting misty-eyed at the thought of so many people crying out to talk to each other and reach some type of common ground.

My e-mail started getting a little less painful to read, too:

"This white male has put Y? Forum in his 'cool' bookmark directory."

"Thank you for providing this forum—too bad people cannot handle honesty such as this face to face."

"Finally! Someone who is exploiting the potential of the web."

"This is a wonderful thing you are doing. Interesting, enlightening, occasionally infuriating. All the things it should be."

"I'm a 15-year-old from a small, mainly white town. I decided to check Y? out, and I was really amazed."

The questions were getting better and better as well. There was Ellen, a white female from New Jersey, who wanted to know what happens in a typical black family household in the evening. Or Tony, a 36-year-old black male from San Francisco, who wondered if white women feared him when he got on an elevator alone with them. Or Mark from Chicago, who was curious about why some gay men talk with a lisp. Or Chris from Florida, who wanted to know where the stereotype came from that Jewish people are thrifty. Or Justin from

Australia, an 18-year-old who asked what people might think when they see he has only one leg.

Or from Cass in Detroit: "Why do white people smell like wet dogs when they come out of the rain?"

I reached the point of no return with that one. It was still early in the project. Some questions had been edgy, but this one . . . *Hmmm,* I thought. *Am I in this for real? Or am I just kidding myself that I can get people to face each other with such frankness?*

I went to Zandria at work and to some other black people I knew. "Is this question for real?" I asked. "Should I post it?"

"Uh, Phil, that's something we talk about," Zandria said. "Yeah, I'd put it up there." From another: "I don't smell it, but a lot of my friends say they have." Another: "Yep, I've heard of it."

To this day, I haven't come across a single black person who isn't familiar with the "rained-on white people smell like wet dogs" phenomenon—or, conversely, a white person who's ever heard of it.

I ended up posting that question, and many more like it. To me, it was symbolic of the whole point of Y?: to get people talking about things they just don't normally talk about. After all, if I can't talk to you about how you smell or speak or wear your hair, how can we sit down over doughnuts and efficiently dissect and solve the world's problems, whether they be about welfare, gay rights, affirmative action, crime, or separation of church and state?

In the end, when people ask me why a straight, white, middle-class married guy raised in an affluent suburb of Chicago would go to such trouble, I can only say this: I don't know a whole lot about a lot of things, and I'm not ashamed to admit it. I've always asked a lot of questions, many of them silly, ignorant, and just plain stupid. I've taken my share of criticism for telling people to do the same. But perhaps it's true that once we admit we don't know something, we're on the path to knowing.

If you're reading this, I'm guessing you believe in that premise. For that, I thank you. I urge you to turn the page and read on.

What you'll find is a sampling of the best questions and responses from among the more than 50,000 posts submitted to Y? so far. In addition, for the book, we stepped things up a notch by soliciting answers from experts and thought leaders on everything from odor to sexual practices to religious customs. And each section ends with a sampling of yet-to-be-answered queries from our users.

In some cases, the comments printed here had to be edited for space or clarity. The full exchange, along with updates, is available at our website. You'll also note that many of our contributors prefer to use nicknames or no name. We ask our online contributors to identify themselves, even if they request to be identified with an alias once we've screened their submission for public posting.

If you haven't done so already, visit Y? at www.yforum.com to add your voice to the sometimes myth-shattering, sometimes hilarious, sometimes heartwarming but never boring dialogue that's recorded in this book. Keeping the conversation going is what this effort has always been about. Because in the end, perhaps the most fascinating, eye-opening aspect of any quest for knowledge is the realization that we might not be alone when we wonder, *Am I the only one who feels like this?*

—Phillip J. Milano

ONE

Color-Bind:

Race
and
Ethnicity

"Why do white people smell like wet dogs when they come out of the rain?"

—CASS, female

Readers Respond

"It can even be nauseating. I've discussed it with a couple of white women I've dated and showered with. They can't smell it (of course) and don't understand it. Neither do I. It seems more pronounced in Europeans. Strangely, it's one of the things that prevents me from continuing to date my Caucasian female friends (to the applause of most of my black female friends)."

—JAMES G., black male

"I haven't noticed that all white people smell like dogs when wet. Maybe you're hanging out with the wrong kind of white people, or maybe your white friends are sleeping with their wet dogs?"

—BOB

"White people may smell like wet dogs if they have been in the rain for the same reason [dogs] smell, although I'd like to think they [dogs] smell worse. The texture of most white people's hair is soft and absorbs a lot of dirt and odors, as does dogs' fur."

—ANONYMOUS

"Given that I've smelled a fair number of wet dogs and also quite a few wet white people, I feel secure in stating white people don't usually smell like wet dogs. Unless, of course, the white person smelled like a dry dog before she/he got wet."

—WILL H., 48

Y? Check

One of our most bewildering questions (at least to white people) proves to be one of the trickier to answer, for the simple reason, as renowned zoologist and olfactory researcher D. Michael Stoddart puts it: "There has been no proper research into such [race and body odor] matters for many decades; that which was reported a century ago was entirely subjective and not substantiated with any chemical analyses, etc. In effect, it was nothing more than the interpretation of one person's nose—a most unreliable and non-representative sensor!"

Pulitzer prize–winning author David K. Shipler, meanwhile, who spent ten years researching and interviewing hundreds of ordinary Americans to complete *A Country of Strangers: Blacks and Whites in America* (Knopf, 1997), notes that the "wet dog" stereotype is one of a series of images some blacks use to describe whites as unclean.

"It's typical in the panoply of images between racial, ethnic, national and religious groups to include lack of cleanliness and subhuman, animal analogies," he says, adding that in the case of African Americans, it might also be a form of "psychological payback" against white bigotry.

While bacteria on the scalp and skin can break down oils to produce a musty odor, especially when wet, there is no evidence Caucasian hair or skin more naturally tends to emit a "wet dog" odor than that of blacks, says Dr. Jerome Z. Litt, a professor of dermatology at Case Western Reserve University School of Medicine who has researched and written extensively about skin and body odor issues over the past fifty years.

"What can happen is that people get 'nose fatigue'—their nose gets used to certain odors of people from their own race, while at the same time they are more sensitive to the smells of people from a different cultural group," says Litt.

And although various factors such as diet and hygiene can contribute to an individual's body odor, Litt dismisses the wet dog descriptor as a "grandmother's tale," adding on a personal note, "My wife is black, and she's never told me I smell that way!"

Stoddart, whose *The Scented Ape: The Biology and Culture of Human Odor* (Cambridge University Press, 1990) reviews the history and science of why humans smell the way they do, concludes that while some generalizations can be made about various odor-producing glands—European males' axillary (armpit) glands are more developed than those of Asian males', for example—overall, "humans have highly individualistic body odors."

Perhaps Litt sums it up best: "When it comes to body odor, it's in the nose of the beholder."

? ? ?

"**I**s it true that black people hoot and holler more at the movies than white people do?"

—YOINKSTA, 15, male

Readers Respond

"Similar patterns of racial differences in vocalization can be seen in the context of worship. Northern Europeans tend to express their appreciation in a quiet and demure fashion. Southern Europeans are more vociferous. Perhaps the warmer the clime and darker the skin, the greater the immediate response to pleasure."

—M.P.

"Surely this is a matter of culture rather than race. To suggest that darker-skinned peoples from warmer climes are naturally more emotional or impulsive is offensive even to my light-skinned, cool-climed self."

—A. MORGAN

"At a Ziggy Marley concert, I experienced the loudest hooting and hollering I've ever heard. That was from the white people. But you will never hear me say that because of their color they have a 'greater reaction' to pleasure."

—JAS, 42, black

"I think this is more about maturity, intelligence and respect for the people around you than it is about race. The individuals who hoot and holler in a theater during the movie come in a variety of colors."

—CARLY

"I am among the lower class of black people, working class to be exact, and I don't hoot and holler at the movie screen. In fact, no one I know does that. A few years ago, my friend and I went to Manhattan to see *Dead Man Walking*. Throughout the movie, the group behind me was talking loudly and making silly comments like 'Look at his hair, it looks stupid.' Guess what? All four were white."

—DENISE, 26, black

Y?Check

"A specific behavior in the black community known as 'loud talk' may give some insight into the way African-American movie audiences behave," says Brenda Rhodes Miller, author of *The Church Ladies' Divine Desserts and Sweet Recollections* (Putnam, 2001) and *The Laying on of Hands* (Doubleday, 2004).

"One of the reasons 'loud talk' exists is that white people seem more likely to expect someone in authority to resolve problems or to manage behavior, whereas black people depend on the group to enforce norms.

"One form of 'loud talk' is to express a personal opinion that represents the feelings of the group. The comment is addressed at high volume to no one in particular, yet often elicits approving responses from the rest of the group.

"If someone skips in a line of black people, someone might speak up and say, 'No, he didn't cut in line!' And the rest of the group will pile on with their comments until the miscreant moves back to his rightful place."

In a movie theater with a black audience, there may be several people who have already seen the movie, while others may think they can predict where the plot will go. Everybody wants to share what they know with the group and may resort to loud talk directed to the characters on screen: "You better watch your back!" "I know what's coming next!" or "Look at that fool going into a dark building in the middle of the night!"

"The 'loud talk' can persist throughout the movie, in a participatory style sharing characteristics with call and response in many worship services," says Miller, wife of a Baptist minister in Washington, D.C.

"It doesn't suit everyone. Fortunately this is a country with room enough for varied worship experiences—as well as any number of movie theaters favored by hooting, hollering audiences."

? ? ?

"During a legal proceeding, a case was presented in which a Hispanic male was co-habitating with a minor Hispanic female. The female was 15 and pregnant by the male. I believe this male is a sexual predator and guilty of sexual assault on a minor. An attorney present stated it was 'a cultural thing' and thus okay. Is an adult male having sex with and impregnating a minor culturally acceptable in Hispanic cultures?"

—G.T.R., 40, white male

Readers Respond

"It is very common in Latin America to see an age difference such as this. When my aunt married my uncle, she was 14 and he was 26. They have been happily married for 25 years. She was 19 when she had her first child. Two years later, she gave birth to another child, and that was it. They were a very healthy and stable family. In Latin America, Hispanics figure the man should be prepared to support his family and the woman should be fertile and able to give a safe birth. Access to medical aid is very low there, so by the time the woman is in her 30s, it gets very dangerous to give birth."

—GENEVA, 19, Hispanic female

"This is never acceptable, and it's not cultural. You don't mention how old the male is, but it still sounds like statutory rape to me."

—ROSANNA, 32, Hispanic female

"It is common to see older Mexican males with younger women. I don't know about Mexicans living in the United States, but here in Mexico it was especially common 50 or more years ago. In Mexico, it's socially wrong when the woman is older than the male in a couple. Women tend to explain this by saying that when they get older, they would seem like the mothers of their husbands. Strange, yes?"

—MIXCOATL, 20, Hispanic male

Y? Check

Some Hispanic and Latino subcultures accept a pairing of a young female with an older man, but not all, according to Los Angeles psychologist Ana Nogales, a native of Argentina and commentator on Hispanic culture and relationships for the Univision network, Telemundo-LA, CNN, and various print media. Much of it has to do with context and custom, she stresses.

"If we go to a more agricultural society, when a girl reaches 15 or 16, she will get married because she is at an age where she can have a family. In that particular society, they are trained to be good wives and mothers. That way, a man can take care of you and be a provider, and the parents can be safe."

Nogales contends that if the man is older, so much the better, because in some cultures he has proven he can survive and prosper, hold a job, and "show he can keep his promises." But such May/December relationships can also be acceptable in bigger cities like Mexico City, though not with a woman so young that she is a minor.

"Women still look in every society at men who have power [and] money . . . not just because women like to have good shoes or purses, but they need to assure that she will . . . have children who will not starve. If we go to a big city like Mexico City, high-class men who have lots of money will also look for younger women because they can show they have a beautiful woman, and that gives him status."

When asked how this custom translates to the United States, Nogales said that it does occur, particularly among new Hispanic or Latino immigrants who cling to the old ways in that they continue with the same values. It will take years to accommodate, or they may never make the adjustment.

If the pairing is between newcomers and is consensual, most in the community "will 'understand' that they fell in love. But when we have it in the first or second generation, that is child abuse," said Nogales.

She also brings up the specter of rape.

"There are many cases of a woman who married at age 15 because she was raped by this guy. She had to marry the rapist because she was ashamed that she was not a virgin anymore," Nogales said. "There are things you don't do here; even if it's OK to do it in your culture, you have to learn to behave in this culture."

? ? ?

"**A S** a black homeowner in a racially mixed subdivision, I've noticed that my Caucasian neighbors spend much more time on lawn care. Do Caucasians see lawn care as basic home maintenance, or is it more of a hobby?"

—CAROLYN L., 36, black female

Readers Respond

"Most of the Caucasian 'lawn freaks' I know, including my husband, are men. If women have that tendency, they seem to become 'garden freaks.' I think white people want their houses to fit in with the care level of their neighbors' houses. They want their lawns to be always green, always trimmed and always weedless to avoid looking like dirtballs by comparison."

—SUSAN K., 51, white female

"I live in an area that is 98 percent Caucasian. The best-looking yard belonged to the only black family in the area. Their yard actually won an award from the town for best-looking lawn."

—HELEN S., 43, white female

"I think white people tend to prefer to control nature as much as they can. This perhaps stems from hundreds of years of doing so. Black people seem to me to seek a more symbiotic relationship with nature, rather than an adversarial one. A well-groomed lawn is simply not natural; having one demonstrates a degree of victory over the natural world."

—JAMES, male

"When a neighborhood is filled with tidy green lawns, we believe it helps promote the overall desirability of the area and keep our home values from eroding. I wouldn't buy a house that looks messy on the outside, because God only knows what's been neglected on the inside."

—KAREN, white female

"I think white culture views a free-standing, single-family home as an important status symbol. A well-kept lawn is part of the package. Maybe this comes from '50s, '60s and '70s sitcoms like *Leave It to Beaver, The Brady Bunch* and *Eight Is Enough*, which showed idealized white families with impossibly perfect lawns."

—STACEE, 30, white female

Y? Check

Failing to find any legitimate scientific researchers exploring Caucasians' lawn-care habits, we settled for the next best thing: pop-culture humorist Stephan Dweck, coauthor of *The Field Guide to White People* (Three Rivers Press, 2000) and the popular *SNAPS* book series of creative African American insults, as well as producer of *The Big Head People,* a cartoon show for the Spike TV network he described as *In Living Color* meets *Southpark*.

Here is his (firmly tongue-in-cheek) reply:

"It is genetically predetermined. Only white people have this neurotic obsession. I'm a city kid. The lawn I have is Central Park. A sure sign of them being obsessed? Look for a white person with tanning lotion. They are inherently multi-taskers, so they want to get a tan while doing the lawn. You don't see black people trying to get a tan while pushing a lawn mower, do you?

"My black friends who do have lawns cut them like they get their Afros cut, once every two weeks. It's not a labor of love. I know some lawns of white people you can eat off of. It's almost like another consumer item: who's got the best lawn, the best car, whose kid is going to the best college.

"I lived in a ritzy suburb once, in Woodbridge, Connecticut, with all white people . . . man those people took care of their lawns. I didn't want to be singled out as the black guy, so I took care of mine. It was racial guilt. I mean, they'd all have lawn meetings at The Home Depot: who's got the best seed, the best fucking flower and dirt . . . hey, if you want to know white America, go to The Home Depot; they're all there. It's like the new church to white people, a new communal ground.

"When I lived in Woodbridge, people would drive by and take pictures of people's lawns! This one guy, his lawn was immaculate, with little statues—no jockeys, but lots of statues. He had all sorts of shit on his lawn, and it was really pretty. It's an extension of 'I'm better than you.'

"Don't get me wrong, in all-black upscale communities, the blacks do that with the lawn, too. They emulate white behavior. But in mixed neighborhoods, it doesn't happen . . . hey, every time I was stopped by the police in Woodbridge, I'd just say I was going to take care of some guy's lawn. They'd let me go."

? ? ?

"At the high school I go to, quite often you see black guys attacking black girls in what appear to be mock rapes. Why do they do that?"

—MICHELLE, 18, Hispanic female

Readers Respond

"What school do you go to? The guys are probably getting a quick feel. Maybe sex with their clothes on, like on the dance floor."

—DOMINANCE, 17, black male

"I teach at an inner-city middle school of almost all black students. I witness this physical play between the boys and girls every minute of the day. When I started, I would give the 'Hey, get off of her' shout to anyone I saw, but after doing that, oh, 10 times in a minute or two, I became blind to it. I think the situation has more to do with the kids' age and sexuality. An older black female teacher told me that most times the girl has done something to lead the boy on before he gets all over her. I can back that up. I see it all damn day. It goes both ways, and it's seen in my Hispanic students, too. I think the problem stems from the combination of hormones and teenage boys' exposure to so many portrayals of women as objects to conquer."

—ERIC, 23, white male

"If the only males you see glorified are those who exhibit aggression, then if you are a male, you will likely emulate that example. The images that black males have to imitate from our culture are not likely to be kind, sensitive and compassionate toward women. Rap, sport [stars] and movie stars are all likely to fit the same profile of aggressiveness. It would help if we provided black males with positive role models, but in order to do that, we as a society of blacks and non-blacks have to value the non-aggressive black males over the aggressive ones."

—C. PHILLIPS, 25, black female

"I saw other white boys around me, especially poor ones, doing this all the time. And girls would squeal and like it. It seemed to be mostly conceited football jocks doing this as a way of letting the girl know, 'Come on, let's do it.' So maybe these black guys have picked it up, too."

—JIM T., 27, white male

"I have often questioned the same thing, and it's wonderful to know other brown-skinned girls notice it, too. I think so many young black men 'play rape' because there is no penalty for doing it. Black women and girls are not highly revered by the dominant culture. When I was in high school, I noticed guys doing the same thing. It was always laughed off, and black girls accepted it as 'any affection from a black man is good affection.' Unfortunately, that belief still exists. It's internalized, racist chauvinism."

—DEVIN, 24, black female

Y?Check

Henry A. Giroux, director of the Waterbury Forum in Education and Cultural Studies at Penn State University, claims that "The specter of these feigned assaults raises issues about the representations of masculinity and black women often found in popular culture.

"Youthful masculinity is increasingly defined through an over-the-top notion of patriarchy, informed largely by an excessive culture of commercialism and a steady stream of hyper-violence," says Giroux, whose research in cultural and youth studies has resulted in books such as *Public Spaces, Private Lives: Beyond the Culture of Cynicism* (Rowman and Littlefield, 2001).

"At the same time, black women—especially in the world of MTV—are increasingly seen simply as bodies and sexual objects. It's not hard to see how these representations limit the possibility of agency for many black males and offer up the most degrading modes of identification for young black women."

Giroux stresses, however, that others' perceptions of such mock rapes might be colored by internalized racist assumptions to begin with, particularly about black male youths, and can serve as an erroneous filter "through which to identify, judge and explain the behavior of black men."

"The notion that black men are pathological rapists has a long history in this country. . . . So the question that was asked needs to be understood within both a larger tradition of racism and the current representations of commercialism, greed and sexism that have become so common in American culture."

? ? ?

"**Why** is it that the most disgusting, crazed and depraved forms of sexuality (incest, being beaten until bruised or scarred, bestiality, being fisted, drinking urine, being defecated upon, necrophilia, etc.) are almost always the province of whites?"

—T. DAVIS, 25, black male

Readers Respond

"Civilization breeds boredom. And for the moment, Western civilization seems to be run by white men."

—ULYSSES N., mixed race male

"I'm sure people of other races do these things, too, but they're smart enough to keep it in the bedroom. White people, on the other hand, like getting caught on tape."

—JEZREEL, 19, Filipina female

"Whites engage in the most disgusting behavior? What about Rick James and his behavior? What about Prince and his, well, everything? What about Michael Jackson? What about Chuck Berry and his 'brown games'? All were African American. All did some pretty weird stuff."

—CARLTON B., 28, white male

"Sex is the main thing that drives evolution, so it seems to me that any race that is more sexually preoccupied has an evolutionary advantage. The more fetishes you have, the more opportunity there'll be for sexual arousal. Therefore, the more perverted a race, the higher its success of continuation. So perhaps white people's pervertedness is just an evolutionary strength that has helped us survive in the past."

—JAMIE, 26, white male

"I don't get it, either. My best guess is that white culture is much less open about sexuality. When you grow up in a culture where nobody talks about sex and it's sort of nasty and dirty to begin with, the taboo of sex itself becomes associated with other taboos. Enjoying sex is then associated with enjoying other bad things—pain, shit, etc. I think Latino and black cultures are more open about sexual desire, and perhaps that's why fewer of them are into kink."

—COLLEEN, 21, white female

Y? Check

If white people have a greater tendency toward deviant or abnormal sexual behavior, it's news to Ted McIlvenna, president of The Institute for the Advanced Study of Human Sexuality in San Francisco. In more than three decades as a sexologist documenting what he calls "more personal sexual histories than anyone in the world,"

McIlvenna says he's found "absolutely no racial differences" when it comes to sexual behavior on the decidedly wilder side.

"What I have found is that the people with the most money and wherewithal to do what they want have better sex lives," said McIlvenna, who holds a doctorate in sexology and helped found the institute, the only graduate school in the country devoted specifically to training sexologists.

More than anything, McIlvenna said, deviant sexual behavior—which he himself brands a pejorative label—has to do with socioeconomic and situational factors, not race. "We don't fuck dead bodies unless we're working in a mortuary, where we would have access. And sticking it in mashed potatoes has mostly to do with whether we go to McDonald's or KFC and whether we can get warm mashed potatoes. It's always about the sexual outlet available."

A good way of looking at it, according to McIlvenna: The more money, time, and opportunity on our hands, the more likely we are to "go there."

? ? ?

"I always hear my black friends call each other 'nigger,' and you hear it in raps, too. Why is it OK when they do it, but if a white person even whispers the word, everyone freaks out, whether they're white or black?"

—HAZE, 23, white male

Readers Respond

"With many African Americans, the N-word is used as a term of endearment or nickname. It's no different from when a person calls their little brother 'Shorty' or 'Stupid' but would get angry if someone outside the family called him those names."

—ANDREA, 36, black female

"As a black person, I'm still trying to understand this. Other blacks may try to justify its use by saying it's a good word for them. The truth is, nobody should use it (not even blacks). How can we justify that we can say something and someone else can't?"

—PETER, 23, black male

"I know white guys who refer to themselves as 'Crackers,' 'Rednecks,' 'Peckerwoods,' 'White Trash,' etc. Same guys would be brandishing a broken beer bottle at someone from another race calling them that. This phenomenon is not limited to African Americans."

—STEVE, 37, white male

"I don't use the word and have never been called one by anyone who did not want my fist to connect with their face. It is degrading and demoralizing. The only blacks I know who use it are of two kinds: 1) They are selfish, narrow-minded and have little respect for other humans, so they don't mind using words that are dehumanizing to anyone, or 2) They grew up in lower economic communities and were influenced by the large commercialism of the rap industry. People in the rap industry use it because it shocks, sensationalizes and turns a buck."

—AMANDA, 19, black female

"In my school there is a large Italian population, so it's not uncommon to hear an Italian referring to another Italian as a 'guido,' 'guida' or 'guidette.' When I first heard them speak like that to each other I was offended, and I'm not even Italian. I think the word 'nigga' is now being used like 'homeboy' or 'homegirl' was in the early '90s. I've seen Italians call each other 'nigga'—and even blacks calling their non-black friends 'nigga.'"

—K.J., 17, black female

Y?Check

Use of 'nigger' or 'nigga' as a term of endearment among some younger African Americans emerged alongside rap and hip-hop music during the post–Civil Rights era of the last two decades, according to Ronald L. Jackson II, associate professor of communication theory at Penn State University and author of *Understanding African American Rhetoric* (Routledge, 2003) and *African American Communication and Identities* (Sage Publications, 2003).

Jackson, an expert on intracultural communication, says that whites—even those in tight-knit groups that include blacks—generally cannot use the term "nigger" to feel connection because so much negative emotion is attached to the word when it is used by a non-black. Some whites are, therefore, angered by what they see as a double standard.

"Some whites may have a sense of entitlement of being able to call people what they want, and to be able to enter into any circle," Jackson says. "It can feel uncomfortable to be restricted. It's not part of their reality on a daily basis."

Geneva Smitherman, University Distinguished Professor of English at Michigan State University who has been at the forefront of African American linguistic studies for more than 20 years, agrees that "nigger," when used by whites, is generally viewed as a racial epithet used to insult or offend a black person.

Because of that, she writes in *Black Talk: Words and Phrases from the Hood to the Amen Corner* (Houghton Mifflin, 2000), it is off-limits to whites: "As the white comic Gary Owen said on a *Def Comedy Jam* show, whites invented the word but can't use it."

? ? ?

"**Why** do black men look good in purple suits, but white men look like dorks?"

—P. RYAN

Readers Respond

"I haven't seen a black man who looked very good in a purple suit. Odds are you will look like a dork by default if you wear one, regardless of race, gender, sexual orientation or religion."

—WAYNE C., 43, black male

"Someone will probably try and give some response about coloring of the skin being complementary or not, so let me try and stop such nonsense before it starts. Most men look good in suits. It may be that you have had more instance to notice a black man in a purple suit because some black men wear colored suits to stand out in a crowd. Being originally from Louisiana, where purple is one of the official state colors, I've had a chance to see several men of both races in purple suits. The better-looking the man, the better-looking the suit."

—AMANDA, 21, black female

"Let's be honest. No one looks good in a purple suit."

—MATT, 26, Hispanic male

"I don't think it's nonsense to state that skin coloring plays a role in what colors look good. A white woman and a black woman are not always able to wear the same color of lipstick and look good in that shade. Therefore, it stands to reason that skin tone makes a difference. Darker skin can carry a brighter (for instance, orange) or deeper color (like purple) better without being overwhelmed by it. Perhaps that's why the colorful Kente cloth patterns were invented by Africans."

—CASSANDRA, 36, black female

Y?Check

Constance White, style director for eBay.com, former style writer for the *New York Times,* and one of the country's best-known fashion journalists, says it's not foolish to think a black man might look better in a purple suit than a white man, for two reasons: color contrast and cultural context.

"Scientifically, we know that black against white is the most graphic you can get, so by the same token the same sort of rules apply to, say, a purple against a brown," says White, who's also followed style for *Elle* magazine and Lifetime Television. "Perhaps to our natural eye it's easier on the eye—darker skin tones balance out a brighter color, whereas a whiter tone would tend to wash it out."

Perhaps as important, "In our community, it's just a lot more acceptable for a black man to wear a purple suit—even if some of us might be rolling our eyes, it's still not as shocking as if a white man shows up in a purple suit to a bar mitzvah or church on Sunday or a WASP party."

White says that tracing that acceptance inevitably leads one on a path back to Africa, where cultural mores and traditions called for the elite leaders to wear bright colors. The contrast with European society was like night and day, with high-profile leaders there wearing very conservative, darker colors.

"There is more of a tradition for individual expression in the black community than in the white community, which comes partly from whites' religious traditions. In Puritanism and the Church of England, they were very buttoned-up. Not only was it not polite in society to express yourself, it was downright ungodly. Whereas in traditional African religions, the opposite is true," White notes.

What also shouldn't be lost on anyone contemplating a color such as purple for a suit is that just as clothes make the man, the man makes the clothes.

"A black man sort of has a swagger that goes with a purple suit, whereas white men don't," White quips. "It's the same reason a 15-year-old model can't carry off wearing an incredible, $30,000 coutured gown. She is just not equipped to wear that in her life experience and make it look its best."

? ? ?

"**Is** it true that most white people wash their hair every day? If I did that, my hair would fall out in clumps because it would be so dry."

—J., 24, black female

Readers Respond

"Most Caucasian people have hair that is finer, straighter and oilier than African Americans' hair. I had a white coworker who only washed his hair once a week, and believe me, it was not a pretty sight."

—CRYSTAL, 30s, white female

"White people's hair gets straggly and stringy and won't do anything if you don't wash it. Mine is kind of dry, so I do it every other day unless I go to the gym. Lots of styles are done using a blowdryer, so you have to get your hair wet, anyway."

—J., white female

"My hair, scalp and face are extremely oily, even by white standards, and if I don't wash it every day (usually twice in a row when I shower) it just feels gross and sticks to my head. If I don't shower at all, it sticks up in all directions—think combination of Don King and Albert Einstein."

—BEN, 24, white male

"If I go longer than 48 hours without washing my hair, it starts to feel greasy. FYI, my mother has an old school textbook from the 1940s on health and hygiene that recommends washing one's hair every two weeks!"

—C.P., 21, white female

Y?Check

On average, white people (especially women) do reach for the shampoo bottle a lot more often than African Americans do.

In surveys for hair-products company Pantene, nine out of ten white women said they wash their hair at least three times a week, and 42 percent said they do it at least seven times a week. But washing that much would be terrible for most African American women's hair, making it brittle and prone to breakage and causing scalp flaking. Almost half of all African American women surveyed said they washed their hair just once or twice a week, and 39 percent said they did it less than once a week.

"African American hair needs so much special treatment, such tender loving care," says Cheri McMaster, a senior scientist at Pantene. She goes on to say that biology and beauty methods both contribute to the differences. White people's scalps typically have more oil glands, making dry hair a smaller problem.

But in addition to having less oil, many African American women use relaxer treatments that dry their hair. To compensate, hair products for black women have much higher levels of moisturizer. Beyond the difference in dryness, whites' hair is usually more symmetrical than African Americans' and, as a result, is less vulnerable to damage.

McMaster concluded that such differences aren't as important to men's hair care, because many men have short, natural styles that are relatively low-maintenance.

? ? ?

"I recently moved to South Boston, or Southie as some call it. Why do the working-class whites seem so racist? I've lived here two months, and I've already heard many comments, and prejudicial actions have been taken against me. One thing that might help—Southie is mostly Irish and Irish-American; maybe they have a history of being this way?"

—KAWAIDA, 17, black female

Readers Respond

"A brief history of racism in Boston: One day in the '70s an ignorant liberal judge trying to analyze a situation he knew nothing about decided it would be a good idea to bus the children from the poorest white school in Boston to the poorest black school in Boston, and vice versa for the black children. Of course, neither white nor black parents wanted to see their children bused across the city to attend school in neighborhoods they knew nothing about, especially when the local school was right up the street. Not knowing who to blame, whites and blacks pitted this horrible social situation against each other, and today the lingering effects of busing can still be observed in the form of racism, not only in Southie, but in almost every ethnic neighborhood in Boston."

—PAUL, 18, Irish American male

"I grew up in Southie. My mom was a lesbian; my brother a gay ballet dancer who hung out mostly with black girls. I attended public school (the Tynan, as opposed to Gatie or St. Peter's), most of my friends were black, and I didn't play hockey or soccer. As you'd expect, I routinely got the shit kicked out of me. I was very 'Southie' in other ways, however. For example, I was racist, deep down. It's a generational thing, passed down from one to the next. Every kid in Southie grows up racist. White kids in the projects hang Tupac posters in their bedrooms but hate 'niggers.' It's, as they say in Southie, 're-donk-ulous.' Anyway, don't take it personally if people give you looks or call you names. They might be acting out because their friends just got robbed by black kids in Dorchester, or their dad was passed over because of 'reverse discrimination' in the fire department, or they're just mildly retarded, which you'll notice a lot of Southie kids seem to be (fetal alcohol syndrome most of the time). Rely on your social instincts and spot a 'good one,' then try to strike up a conversation."

—JOE, 23, white male

Y? Check

South Boston's racial attitudes have been a subject of commentary in New England for many years. Census records show the neighborhood remained almost monolithically white for decades. Controversy about busing to desegregate schools in the 1970s helped focus national attention on Southie. In 1976, when youths from South Boston and Charlestown protested busing outside Boston City Hall, one of the teens used an American flag to stab a black businessman. The moment was captured in a Pulitzer prize–winning photo.

Irish immigrants in South Boston displayed antiblack feelings almost as soon as they arrived in the nineteenth century, according to Thomas O'Connor, a South Boston native and history professor at

Boston College whose books include *South Boston: My Hometown* (Northeastern University Press, 1994) and *The Hub: Boston Past and Present* (Northeastern University Press, 2001).

They also had a fierce determination to hold their neighborhood in the face of any outsiders, even Irish from other parts of South Boston. Many had been evicted from their homes in rural parts of Ireland, and O'Connor says that might have affected them as they banded together in patrols that challenged outsiders coming into their turf.

"They were homeless. They got here and, by God, you weren't going to move them again," he says. "They clung to their neighborhoods. They clung to their homes."

O'Connor says that among a long list of outsiders, blacks were not only the easiest to spot, but like the Irish, they were at the bottom of America's economic ladder, and both groups wanted to move up.

South Boston's geography also insulates the neighborhood. It's a peninsula reached by bridges, making it harder to quietly diversify a neighborhood a block at a time. O'Connor says physical isolation is a main difference between South Boston and other Northern communities, such as the Irish enclaves in the movie *Gangs of New York,* where ethnic identity vanished or eroded generations ago.

But time has not stood still in Southie. The neighborhood is being discovered by more outsiders, often attracted by its relative safety and comparatively modest real estate prices.

"You will find much more diversity. You will find people of color. There are yuppies and hippies," O'Connor says. "For a long time there were only the natives of South Boston."

? ? ?

"**Why** is it that black women who are overweight exude self-confidence, while most white overweight women hate themselves and try desperately to change their bodies?"

—JENNIE, 22, white female

Readers Respond

"As a black woman who has been overweight most of my life, I can say that one reason for the confidence is that our men seem to prefer our curves—they tell us that they prefer a curvy size 9 to a skinny size 6. They say they prefer a slightly rounded belly to seeing our rib bones sticking out. As long as we are proportional and healthy, we make the cut. Also, we did not necessarily internalize the national/international standard of beauty because it did not include us—but this is changing. Bulimia and anorexia nervosa are increasing in young black teens at an alarming rate."

—TINU, 27, black female

"I think African-American women are stronger, socially, than most. They've had to be. More than any other group in our country, these women have had to overcome the most trials and prejudice. I'm tired of society having unrealistic concepts of what women should look like. Look how many women we've lost because of this. We need to love ourselves—no matter what our size."

—CYNDI, 28, white female

"In black culture it is definitely not cool to be supermodel-thin. When I was younger I was always teased for being skinny and always had relatives trying to get me to eat. Big hips, chests and behinds are prized among most black men. As a result, heavy black women are comfortable with their weight."

—K.J., 17, black female

"Confidence comes from inside, when you realize that you will never be what fashion magazines want but can still acknowledge that you are 'all that' because you look in the mirror and can see it. You learn to carry your confidence well and have no shame for being who you are."

—MRS. WILLIAMS, 28, black female

Y ? C heck

There's no sense even trying to paraphrase L.A. comedian René Hicks, who gave us the skinny on the long-held belief that black women love to be "large and in charge." Hicks's blunt style has served her well on numerous cable TV comedy specials and on college campuses nationwide, where she devotes a good chunk of her act to blowing up stereotypes and forcing audience members to face their differences head-on.

Here's her take:

"Yeah, black women tend to carry more fat, and we're structured differently than white women. But even though black women walk around going 'It's OK to be overweight,' it's only because the pressure is not necessarily on them to hold up the banner of what is considered the epitome of beauty in this country—the Halle Berry standard set up by white folks.

"But think about it: When a black man gets really successful, the first thing he does is go out and get a trophy wife, and he gets what's close to that white beauty standard. Rarely do you see them come up with some big fat black woman, do you? And black women don't like it, believe me. I've heard it.

"You want to know why there's this acceptance of big black women? It isn't necessarily that they accept it themselves; it's that the majority of society is more comfortable with a black woman who gives off the old 'mammy' image or the 'big church sista' image: 'Oh look, it's the jolly fat black woman!'

"These women may act confident, but on the inside, when she's home on Saturday night alone again with no date, she's crying. Look at Oprah. She made it as a big black woman, but look how she struggles to *not* be a big black woman now. Was she confident when she was fat? Maybe. Did she like it? No. She wouldn't spend all this money on special trainers and diets if she did.

"Some of it also has to do with the fact that we've been cultivated to eat foods to make us fat, all the way from slavery—we ate what the slavemaster gave us. Hell, when I was growing up I ate what my mother gave me. We weren't educated to cut out the fried foods and the pork. It's like, my mom would have put pork in Jell-O if you'd let her: 'Hey, it's a meal *and* a dessert! Pretend they're marshmallows!'

"But even though we don't like being fat, we *can* get away with being a little larger. Black men do like a little more booty, and maybe a little more on the top. And so we are more comfortable being some-what bigger. These white women are starving themselves to look like Ally McBeal. They need to eat. How does a man think he's going to have sex with them if they look like they could play hula-hoop with a Cheerio? I mean, the guy would need to hit that thing dead-on if he wanted to make love, you know what I mean? Like threadin' a needle."

? ? ?

"The adults in all three Asian-American families in my neigh-borhood seem very anti-social. Their very Americanized kids seem 'nor-mal,' but the parents won't even make eye contact. Is there some social rule I'm not aware of?"

—S.B., 38, white

Readers Respond

"Many adult Asian immigrants don't speak English very well and, therefore, seem anti-social. My grandmother, for example, is very self-conscious about her English and would feel very strange in the presence of people who don't speak Cantonese. Therefore, she would rather stay at home or keep quiet than 'embarrass herself' by saying the wrong thing."

—CYNTHIA, 19, Chinese female

"My maternal great-grandfather was Japanese, and my family has lived in Japan a long time. I have noticed the same non-eye contact you mentioned, as it is part of the concept of politeness in Japan. It is considered impolite and aggressive to make eye contact with someone, unless that person is a family member, a close friend or of lower status than you."

—A. GOODE, 20, white female

"I think they are just afraid. Asian (especially Chinese) immigrants coming to the United States in the last decade or so have always isolated themselves because they feel white people discriminate against them. It is also cultural. Unlike Americans, they are more reserved and may not feel comfortable expressing their thoughts so openly to people outside their families. On top of that, they may also have a language problem, which makes it worse. A loud, friendly, typical American may intimidate them a bit. So avoidance and isolation is the best choice. That's why there are so many Chinatowns in the United States. They may appear to be unfriendly on the surface, but they may be different on the inside."

—ANONYMOUS

"Many Asian societies do find direct eye contact very disrespectful. It's especially evident when dealing with authority. For example, recently immigrated Asian students of mine never look me directly in the eye because I am in a higher position as the teacher. It's something I've had to adjust to because I grew up more Americanized, and I always thought of direct eye contact as a sign of honesty, straightforwardness and respect."

—K.S.P., 27, Asian female

Y?Check

There aren't cultural rules against socializing, but there are barriers, especially for immigrants who aren't totally comfortable with life in the United States. Language is the most obvious hurdle and one that's different for different generations. Of 7.7 million Asian American adults counted in the 2000 U.S. Census, 43 percent weren't fluent in

English. But three-fourths of the kids were fluent, and 30 percent spoke only English.

Tuyet Le, executive director of the Asian American Institute in Chicago, says that even many immigrants with a good command of the language underestimate themselves and worry they'll make mistakes during conversation.

"Sometimes it's easier for people to let their children interact," Le says. "A lot of times their children are sort of their ambassadors, which isn't always appropriate."

That will vary family to family, as will their general comfort with American culture. Some planned for years to come to the United States and deliberately prepared, while others were refugees who ended up in America almost by chance.

And even when people plan all along to live in America, it takes courage to live in a community with different rules and social norms. "There is a totally different kind of interaction with non-Asians or people not from your native country," Le says.

? ? ?

"I am a 36-year-old black male with a shaved head and goatee. I am 6'1" and weigh 175 pounds. Would I be frightening to a woman alone with me in an elevator? What about walking on a downtown sidewalk after 6 P.M.?"

—TONY W., 36, gay black male

Readers Respond

"I would likely be very uncomfortable because you are a lot bigger than I am. I have to admit your race would add to my discomfort somewhat, because I'm still unlearning childhood prejudices picked up in the white, rural community I grew up in. The prevailing attitude was that we should be afraid of blacks because they were all criminals, even though all the local crime was committed by the white people who lived there. Pretty stupid, huh?"

—HEIDI J., 31, white female

"As a middle-aged woman who grew up in this violent society, I can assure you I'm very nervous about getting into an elevator alone with any man I don't know."

—BECKY, 50, white female

"I think a woman would be scared because people and the news make it sound like black people are real bad and that if you look at them wrong they will kill you or hit you in the mouth or something like that. So it makes people think all black people are bad."

—JEFF, male

"I am a female martial artist who has been interested in women's safety and self-defense for a number of years. It doesn't matter what you look like because women are told that the most sweet-looking man can be a rapist or murderer. If you have experienced fear from a woman in an elevator or on a deserted sidewalk after dark, it was probably more because you were a man than because of your race, height or appearance. Try not to take it personally. You could try getting out of the elevator yourself, or purposely keeping your distance if you encounter a woman in an isolated place. Many of us view that as the modern version of chivalry."

—D.B., female

Y? C heck

Gauging threats posed by strangers can be a necessary but unsettling exercise in snap judgments. Brent Staples, a *New York Times* journalist with a Ph.D. in psychology, has written about the way people often scurried to avoid him when they saw his large, African American frame walking down the street at night. (He found that whistling Beethoven eased people's anxiety.)

But fear varies from person to person, and figuring out what provokes it is tricky.

"When we try to take a template and stick it on an individual, it creates a lot of problems," says Hannah Scott, a criminologist at the University of Ontario Institute of Technology. "It is like trying to see into the center of a house. Your view changes depending on what window you are looking through."

A person's race, gender, and age all have some effect on how they're perceived. A 2000 study by University of Wisconsin–Madison researchers found people considered neighborhoods more crime-ridden when they saw young black men around, even if crime statistics didn't support their view. Even African Americans believed to a lesser degree that crime must be higher in those neighborhoods.

Women are more likely to say they're afraid of violent crime, even though young men more often report they've experienced violence. Research also suggests a lot of women's fears are tied to anxiety about sexual violence. When she reviewed a national survey of Canadian women, Scott found almost a third said they had been frightened by a stranger following them, and about that many sometimes deliberately avoided walking past men or boys.

Scott says that a lot of factors, from a woman's cultural background to how much television she watches, might influence how she'd regard a man in an elevator. Since there's no way to see into the stranger's mind, the best advice is to act compassionately and think about how the world might look through another's eyes.

? ? ?

"Why do people from India haggle so much? I am in retail sales, and I work in an industry where margins are low. I have come very close to losing my temper with people who haggle like this."

—DOUG, white male

Readers Respond

"In many cultures, paying the marked price is considered a sucker's game. The haggling is sometimes very straightforward, and sometimes it is an oblique part of sharing a cup of tea and conversation. I'm barely old enough to remember when haggling was done in many shops in the United States, and it is still done in some places (consumer electronics, for example). For someone who takes haggling for granted, they may take your refusal to do so as a lack of respect."

—JERRY S., 54, Jewish male

"In most shops in India, if you bargain with the store owner, you might get a discount. That's because most shops here are small operations, not big supermarkets like in the United States."

—JATIN, 32, Indian male

"I am a manager in the customer service industry, and most of the time that we have a problem customer, it is a Hindu or similar. I believe it is cultural, but I can't stand them anyway, so I always send one of my subordinates to deal with them. I have no patience for such nonsense."

—RICK, 41, white male

"India's a pretty poor country, and people have always been taught to save as much as they can. Next time, just tell them the price is fixed and you will not accept any price less."

—PRATICHI, 18, Indian female

"Back in the Homeland (Middle East, India, Bangladesh or whatever) the economy and marketing strategies are very different. You will see two salespeople, for example, selling shoes, sitting right next to each other. There is no such thing as a fixed price, so they are in a position to begin with a higher price and reduce it later on the spot and still get a profit. When a patron comes by, he or she will obviously try to haggle the price down. It's just something most of these people are used to and is accepted by the culture. They just have to get used to the fact that the way things are done here is different."

—J.K., 22, Indian male

"I've been to a lot of places where bargaining is expected. That's the way it is here in Israel. It's just that in the United States it's not done that way, and you have no experience dealing with it. The foreigners you deal with instinctively feel that the price you quote is an outrageously overpriced opening bid and expect it to come down."

—JESSE N., 41, male

Y?Check

To Ed Brodow, a nationally recognized negotiation expert and motivational speaker, one might just as well ask, "Why don't Americans like to haggle more?"

"We used to be terrific hagglers during the days before World War II, but our economic success has created a negative connotation for negotiation of any kind," says Brodow, author of *Beating the Success Trap* (HarperCollins, 2003) and *Negotiate with Confidence* (Amer Media). "We are suffering from our own prosperity."

He went on to note that culturally speaking, it is important to remember that in India it is not just acceptable to haggle, but it is even considered foolish not to try to get the best possible deal.

"The person from India offers an important contribution to American culture by reminding us that negotiation is an integral part of our capitalist system," Brodow says. "Americans who find this behavior aggravating are failing to recognize that each of us has the right to negotiate."

Instead of getting upset over the haggling, Brodow suggests developing a better understanding of other cultures and taking courses to obtain better negotiation skills, "which are undoubtedly lacking."

That's not to say Indians who come to this country don't also need to develop some sensitivity to cultural differences in the United States, to soften their behavior when interacting with Americans.

"Ultimately, one of the benefits we derive from our diverse cultural melting pot is that we can expand our capabilities and knowledge by learning what other cultures have to teach us. In this case, the lesson is that we need to be more assertive," Brodow says.

? ? ?

"**Do** black people who have thick lips kiss better than people with thin lips? In other words, is it more fun to have more lip?"

—H.B.G., 55, white male

Readers Respond

"As a matter of fact, it is. I've kissed my share of large-lipped women. There is more movement and manipulation with women whose lips are larger. A lot of fun."

—ELLIOTT, black male

"The chemistry between the people involved determines how enjoyable a kiss is, not the size of the lips."

—SUNSHINE, black female

"I am a 35-year-old black man with nice, full lips. I have always been told I was a great kisser, by both black and white women. Most told me it was because my lips were so full."

—PAUL, black male

"The question of whether thick lips are more enjoyable is more of a personal preference. I am attracted to thick lips, no matter what the person's ethnic or racial mix, and tend to enjoy them more when kissing. It seems to be a greater sensation, probably because there's more surface area. But being a good kisser doesn't require having thick lips."

—ROB, 33, gay white male

Y? Check

Michael Christian, who's surveyed more than 100,000 people on smooching in the United States and 23 foreign countries since 1989, says fuller, fleshier lips can certainly come in handy at kissing-time.

Christian, who wrote *The Art of Kissing* (St. Martin's Press, 1999) under the pen name William Cane, also said that the lips are an erogenous zone, serving as a primary signal of the potential for oral pleasure—and the larger that signal, the easier for others to perceive such a potential.

"With more lip, there are going to be more nerve impulses, so maybe there's a little more advantage to poutier lips," he said. "However, any normal human has so many nerve endings in the lips and tongue that they're going to have a terrific time kissing, whether their lips are full or just plain."

Although Christian hasn't found that African Americans have more fun kissing (not all, of course, have larger lips, anyway, he noted), he has discovered a spectrum in the quantity and style of kissing across continents. Asians, for instance, appear to do the least amount of kissing, while North Americans are somewhere in the middle, and Europeans, especially those near the Mediterranean in the south, pucker up most frequently.

The stampede by movie stars to medical offices for collagen injections sets a bad example, Christian says, because the procedure is painful and needs to be done repeatedly to keep the lips full.

Besides, he says, kissing is erotic enough—Freud even called it a form of "perversion" because it involved an act that is essentially unnecessary for procreation—that everyone can enjoy it naturally.

"Yes, large lips are essentially pleasurable to see and a nice visual cue, but we don't want to make people with thin lips feel left out. There's a place for them."

? ? ?

"**Why** do Asian people persist in using chopsticks (especially in the United States) when knives, forks and spoons are available and so much easier to use?"

—DAVID H., 31, white male

Readers Respond

"Try using one, and only one, eating utensil to shovel down chicken, rice, noodles, beef, fruit and finger foods. You can use a fork to pick a chicken leg, but using a spoon for it would be silly. You can use a fork to roll up noodles, but with a spoon, the noodles just fall over. I can do all of the above with one utensil—the chopstick. I can also manufacture a chopstick with my own hands wherever I can find wood. I can't forge a tin fork and spoon that easily."

—DAVID L., 27, Asian American male

"I think it's because they have extreme problems assimilating into Western culture. They tend to associate with only other Asians, and they speak their Asian languages in their homes for two, three and four generations. They feel that the use of chopsticks sets them apart from the rest of society."

—JIMMY K., 20, black male

"There is no law saying Asians and Asian Americans must give up part of their culture because they are in the United States."

—NICOLE W., 20, black female

"I grew up using chopsticks, and I think they are elegant and very intelligent utensils. Instead of stabbing your food with a fork, we pick up the food delicately between two chopsticks. Most Asian foods are delicately put together and do not lend themselves to be mauled apart by knives and forks. For example, how would you eat sushi with a knife and fork? I guess you can, but you would destroy the whole point of sushi—it should be eaten in one bite. Almost all our foods are prepared so that they are already bite-size when served on the table, so there's no need to cut. All that is done in the preparation stage, in the kitchen. In that sense, I think knives and forks are less efficient and cumbersome."

—CINDY, 25, Asian female

Y?Check

Chopsticks have been the utensil of choice in parts of Asia for thousands of years. Confucius, the great philosopher of the sixth and fifth centuries B.C., warned that an "honorable and upright man allows no knives on his table," apparently because of their association with violence.

Cathy Bao Bean, whose family immigrated from China when she was a child and who wrote about navigating two cultures in *The Chopsticks-Fork Principle: A Memoir and Manual* (We Press, 2002), claims that for Asian-Americans, the correct table utensils depend on where one is dining and how the food is served.

"If I was served rice on a plate, then a fork or spoon—with a little pushing action from the knife—would get the food to my mouth with the least amount of spill," she says. "On the other hand, if the rice was served in a small bowl at a dinner where lifting the bowl to one's lips was considered OK by the Empress Dowager's protocol officer, then pushing the rice directly into my mouth with chopsticks could be considered the 'better' method under these particular circumstances."

Bao Bean says Asian cuisine, especially Chinese, has features that make knives unnecessary. On the premise that guests shouldn't be expected to prepare their meals, Chinese chefs chop food into bite-size pieces or cook it so thoroughly that there's no need for cutting. Food is served hot, and wooden or ivory chopsticks have the benefit of not conducting heat or altering the dish's flavor.

Meals promote a sense of community, so the typical Chinese dining table is round and free of the floral centerpieces or other adornments found in some American homes.

"Everyone leans into the table or stands up to serve an elder or honored guest a delicious morsel from one of the family-style dishes located as centrally as possible, all the while repeating or listening to the same story just in case someone didn't hear it the first or second time around," Bao Bean notes. "To facilitate this criss-crossing togetherness, form follows function. No one should be concerned about knocking extraneous tableware to the floor, taking the last piece of chicken or having to rubberneck around flowers or candlesticks that block the view. A 'quiet Chinese meal' is an oxymoron."

? ? ?

"I know a disproportionately large number of Italian-American families with houses filled with rococo furniture, clear vinyl-covered carpets and furniture, loud wallpaper, yards covered in statuary and fountains, initials on the garage door, large Cadillacs with aftermarket vinyl roofs in the driveway, ornate wrought-iron fences surrounding the property, elaborate shrines to the Virgin Mary, and so on. Why are these tastes so prevalent among them?"

—DAVE, white male

Readers Respond

"Most Italian immigrants came from poor backgrounds in southern Italy, where home ownership was not possible. They worked hard in the United States and wanted to visibly express the joy of home ownership and its related possessions. Many had a flamboyant nature, and their homes expressed this trait. I'm second generation, a college-grad executive type, live in a beautiful house on a two-acre wooded setting, and have never owned a Caddy. I owe it all to a hard-working father with a fifth-grade education and devoted mother who insisted I go to college. We descendants of those immigrants also joke about those gaudy things you mentioned. And now we watch others, newly arrived in this country, do similar things. It's part of this beautiful thing we have called America. By the way, you forgot to mention gold chains with horns and diamond pinky rings!"

—DAVE E., 47, Italian American male

"Maybe the gaudiness comes from the American part of Italian-American. After all, the Italian side can boast of Raphael, da Vinci, Michelangelo, Bernini, Pirandello, etc. I'm Italian-American, and my taste runs to Post-Impressionism and Art Deco. Go figure."

—LAURA O., 38, Italian American female

Y?Check

Bad taste is universal, but ostentatious furnishings, a hallmark of some Italian American homes, are "probably less common" in the Old Country itself, says Roberta Barazza, who teaches English and German at Liceo Artistico Statale in Treviso, Italy.

"It is worth considering that those who emigrated, especially in the past, to the United States were sometimes people with less money and less education in general," says Barazza, who has written for such publications as *Il Mensiliano, Il Friuli,* and *Il Libretto.*

One of the things they might have taken with them to their new country was knowledge of Italian bureaucracy, which likes to complicate things instead of preferring simplicity, she notes.

"We sometimes consider Americans naive for certain simplicity, but you can consider us often uselessly complicated. In universities you can see this: papers and papers of complicated theories which are often completely useless but give an impression of 'high complexity.' "

In fact, when she was studying in Austria, a professor there offered this definition of Barazza's homeland: "Italy is a big theater. A lot of external show of anything, but this only covers emptiness of real action and real result."

Whether that's true is open to debate, but Barazza says she thinks the description fits. So when adapting to a culture that is typically more open and less strict and cold, Italian immigrants to the United States might see their over-the-top decorations as a way to blend in, Barazza surmises.

? ? ?

"Does it hurt that much to be an African American?"

—REV. J. O'DAILY, 38, male

Readers Respond

"It depends on where you live. I grew up in Boston—probably one of the most segregated and racist cities in the United States. Life was hard—fighting for a decent education, job, place to live—life seemed unbearable."

—ROCHELLE, 33, black female

"It hurts a lot. Unless you are an African American, you can't know what it's like. You walk into a store, and they already know you want to steal something so they've got their eyes on you all the time. Just walking down the street, everyone I meet could be the former owner of something I stole, so they don't even want to look at me. But, maybe I didn't steal from them. Then the cops want to haul me in for just about anything because I look like somebody else. It's everywhere, and I can't get away from it."

—GARY, black male

"I don't run into as much outright hate as my grandparents and parents did. I think of them being told they were lower than whites—having it pushed in their faces would make it painful. Or being put down based on something you cannot change: your skin color. It would also hurt to see that no matter how well you raise your child, they will never do as well in life as a white child raised the same way."

—EBONY, 23, black female

Y? Check

Deborah Mathis, nationally syndicated columnist and author of *Yet a Stranger: Why Black Americans Still Don't Feel at Home* (Warner Books, 2002), recalls a recent incident in which her college-aged son called from the road and mentioned that his taillight was out.

"I said, 'Go now—get it fixed. Right now.' Without even processing what he had told me, the first thing I thought of was this young black man, his hair in dreads, the rap music on, sitting in his car with loose-fitting clothes and not looking like Tiger Woods . . . for a lot of people, that represents trouble, and I didn't want him to give some cop an excuse to pull him over."

This awareness of the "race thing" by African Americans "festers on a low boil all the time," Mathis says. Most of the time it registers as background noise, sometimes it's an annoyance or irritation, and occasionally it leads to full-blown hurt or anger.

Sometimes such "radar" for detecting ill intentions can go awry, she admits, as when she assumed a white flight attendant wanted to see her boarding pass because of doubts Mathis should be in first class, when in fact the attendant wanted to hang it on Mathis's coat for ID purposes at the end of the trip. "You get so accustomed to it being the other thing [bias] that sometimes you're off."

She goes on to say that the point, though, is that black people's antennae are constantly up, ready to pick up signals and ward off wrongdoing. Although most African Americans write off their more routine experiences with prejudice, the accumulation of real or suspected oppression "wears your soul down . . . how many of these situations put together do there need to be before they take over your being?"

Mathis gives other examples of insulting behavior: Her friend, an assistant provost at Vanderbilt University, was asked while shopping where he got his platinum MasterCard; a convenience store clerk commanded her son to display his money "the second he set his foot in the door"; and a D.C.–area high school student caught doodling in class was taken to the principal's office and accused of writing gang graffiti.

"So much rolls off our backs, you wouldn't believe it. The little indignities, nasties, people wouldn't believe."

African Americans must each choose how to live with such obstacles, she adds. Some arm themselves with information, others blow it all off, others get angry, and still others just get in your face.

"For example, a black kid came on the Metro [subway in Washington] the other day, singing loudly along with a CD with his headphones on, and he's just going 'Mothafucka, so and so . . .' He knew what he was doing was disturbing and rude, and that's why he did it," she says. "If he wants to join Future Farmers of America and they say no, or he goes out for the football team and they say no, or he gets a detention, he has no power, but God-damnit, he has the power to shake you up, and for him, fear is a reasonable substitute for respect."

Ultimately, Mathis says, she feels the majority of people, whatever race, want to do the right thing, but the amount of wrong-headed actions has led blacks to develop a sixth sense and to frequently question motives.

"We've been fed so much poison that it's hard to see clearly now. Some may think our complaining is just out of habit. I assure you it is not. We've got other things to do. I'd love to be spending my energy on something else."

Still in Question

A Sampling of Race- and Ethnicity-Related Questions
Seeking Answers at Y? (www.yforum.com)

"Why don't white people use tissues or handkerchiefs instead of their bare fingers to clean their noses?"

—M.

"Why are most black people afraid of the woods?"

—CHRISTOPHER L., 25, white and Latino male

"Why do Italians use their hands so much when they speak?"

—MELODY, 34, white female

"Why do a lot of people of Asian descent own black hair care products stores? What do they know about black people's hair?"

—NAOMI, 20, black female

"Why do black people eat so much cheese doodles and drink grape soda?"

—TOAST, 24, white male

"I've always wondered why it seems the majority of older Spanish/Mexican men gawk at females who walk by and even call out to them with lewd gestures and whistles."

—J. WU, 18, Asian female

"I work for an older, wealthy, Jewish woman. I am taken aback when she walks into our office and begins criticizing everything. I've been told this trait is typical of Jewish women. Is there any truth to this?"

—ANONYMOUS, 30

"How do white people feel about the phrase 'white trash'?"

—N.P., 35, African American male

"What is the origin and significance in Hispanic culture of weeping until one passes out after the death of a loved one?"

—J. COOK, 43, white

TWO

Beyond Beliefs:

Religion

"I am told it is impossible for men not to ejaculate at least once in a while; that if they don't, the sperm just builds up. So how do priests deal with this? If they don't masturbate, do they wait for a wet dream? And are both of these, or either of these, considered to be 'impure thoughts' and therefore a sin?"

—SALLY C., 23, white female, raised Catholic

Readers Respond

"Back in Catholic school, I was taught that masturbation was a sin. Like most Catholic men (and health professionals), I thought that was completely silly and ignored the rule. Still do. Just as all the Catholic women I know use birth control, even though it is also considered a sin. Wet dreams, on the other hand, have no taint of sin around them. Catholicism does not hold people accountable for their dreams. If a man goes without sex or masturbation for a few days or weeks, he will almost certainly have a wet dream. He may or may not remember it the next day. (Mind you, I know about four Catholic priests, most of whom are gay and have partners. So I suppose they don't have this problem. And yes, that's considered a sin, too.) I think in general, perhaps you are expecting priests to be more strict about the details of religion than they really are."

—JOHN, 36, gay white male, Catholic

Y? Check

The bottom line: Most priests self-pleasure themselves, says retired Catholic priest A.W. Richard Sipe, regarded as the nation's foremost authority on the psychological and spiritual aspects of celibacy.

"Catholic priests are required to bind themselves by a promise of 'perfect and perpetual' chastity; in spite of this promise, the vast majority of priests masturbate at least occasionally. Some priests use pornography in connection with masturbation," says Sipe, a psychotherapist whose research and conclusions are based on 25 years of interviewing more than 2,000 priests worldwide.

An author of several books on celibacy, including *Sex, Priests and Power: Anatomy of a Crisis* (Brunner/Mazel, 1995) and *A Secret World: Sexuality and the Search for Celibacy* (Brunner/Mazel, 1990), Sipe says the Catholic Church teaches that it is a grave sin for anyone to stimulate himself or herself to the point of orgasm, and his research found that many priests do maintain a celibate lifestyle "for more or less long periods of time." Still, "some do not feel that masturbation destroys their commitment, but is necessary and natural," he says.

As far as wet dreams, or nocturnal orgasms, they are natural occurrences in men and women who aren't sexually active and are more common during youth. There is generally "no moral significance attached to their incidence," Sipe says.

As a final note, Sipe adds that although masturbation may be the most common sexual activity of priests, it is not the only sexual outlet for many: His 25-year study revealed that at any one time, "no more than 50 percent of priests are maintaining their celibacy." Other forms of sexual activity of priests, he says, "can include more or less long-term sexual relationships with women or men, or experimental, dating types of relationships with either sex."

? ? ?

"**I**s it true that Hassidic Jews must have a sheet between them (with a hole cut in it) while having sexual intercourse? If so, why?"

—SINGLE WHITE FEMALE

Readers **R**espond

"Some Orthodox Jews have special prohibitions about women's bodies, hair and functions, and these are often also the groups that, for example, only permit intercourse through a hole in the sheet. Please note that this is not mainstream Judaism, just like a prohibition on dancing is not mainstream Christianity."

—A.B., Reform Jew

"I am not a Hassidic Jew, but I'm certainly familiar with Jewish law, and my grandparents started out Hassidic. Unless they have some secret practice not shared by or known to other Jews, this sheet story is poppycock. It may be that this is a distorted version of an actual practice. According to Jewish law, a menstruating woman is ritually unclean and may not physically touch or be touched by a man. Once her period is over, she will undergo a cleansing ceremony and can then interact normally with her husband. While she is unclean, a wife and husband will sleep in separate beds to avoid both accidental contact and temptation. (In fact, she will avoid doing anything to encourage displays of affection, such as making his favorite food.)"

—JERRY S., 52, Jewish male

Y?Check

Jewish law not only does not mandate a sheet be placed between a couple during sex, it pointedly calls for no clothing to be worn during lovemaking, according to Rabbi Shmuley Boteach, author of a number of books, including *Kosher Sex: A Recipe for Passion and Intimacy* (Doubleday, 1999).

The ancient rabbis held that "sex must bring in its wake this tidal wave of powerful emotion that leaves a couple feeling closer, and this happens specifically through the powerful emotions awakened when the body is caused to tingle by contact with another body," Boteach writes in *Kosher Sex.*

Rabbi Reuven Eliyahu, a Torah scholar and researcher for Ohr Somayach Tanenbaum College in Jerusalem, says the Talmud (Tractate Ketubot 48a) states that the insistence of one spouse for an intervening garment would be grounds for divorce, and this is codified as Jewish Law in the Shulchan Aruch (Even Haever 76:13).

The "hole-in-the-sheet" misconception, which has become a part of Jewish lore related to the strictness of Orthodox practices, might have several origins, Eliyahu says. One has to do with the fact that some observant Jews wear a tallit katan (little tallit), a large, white, square piece of material that is worn like a T-shirt under the outer clothing. It has a hole in the middle for the head and strings on each corner. "Now, what does a tallit katan look like, clipped to the clothesline by one edge and hanging fully flat?" Eliyahu says. "That's right, it looks like a sheet with a hole in the middle. Hence the widespread misconception that Jews use sheets with holes in them."

The myth might also have gained fuel from another biblical verse (Deuteronomy 22:17) that says the father "spreads out the sheet" to prove that his daughter was indeed a virgin on her wedding night. One interpretation of this phrase, Eliyahu says, is that in biblical times "witnesses were on hand outside the room for the first time that the bride and groom were alone together. Blood on the sheet upon which the bride and groom lay was considered evidence of her chastity." This is not practiced today, Eliyahu notes, and "Either way, Jews do not sleep with holey sheets."

? ? ?

"I've seen it reported in the media that a male who dies fighting for Islam goes to Heaven and gets some large number of virgins (70?). So I always wonder what the incentive is for Islamic women to behave."

—LESLIE, agnostic white female

Readers Respond

"Rights and responsibilities of men and women in Islam are divided so that they reach an equilibrium. An accusation often made against Muslims is that the Quran says men have been made stronger than women to be able to handle certain responsibilities. This is not discrimination, but a fact of nature, that a man is physically stronger than a woman, but the best of people is decided on faith and not whether they are a man or a woman. In regard to women in heaven, they are called Hurs, and believing women will be given men, called Ghilman. So there is no difference in that."

—ZUHAIR R., 20, Asian male, Muslim, United Arab Emirates

"The distinct property of heaven in the Quran is that it is a place of fulfillment. In essence, heaven is what you want it to be. If you want it to be a place where you leave your bodily form and become one with the universe, then so be it. If it is a place filled with fairy-like companions or studs, then so be it. If a woman wants her heaven to be in the form of a sex machine, so be it! No Muslim believes heaven is for men only. The reward is equal, and the requirements to receive this reward are equal. The myth of a masculine Muslim heaven filled with a fixed number of virgins per faithful is one of the most inane yet widespread misunderstandings about Islam. When someone dies in my country, people see that person as being 'with God,' not in bed with virgins. To think otherwise is to grossly underestimate the complex feelings millions of Muslims have about an issue as convoluted as death and what happens after it."

—KARIM, 23, Arab male, Muslim, Cairo, Egypt

Y? Check

That would be 72 virgins, to be exact—but the entire notion of such a prize waiting in heaven for Muslim men has been "blown out of proportion," says Sayyid Muhammad Syeed, Secretary General of the Islamic Society of North America.

The "promise" is not even mentioned specifically in the Quran and might instead stem from a quotation of the Prophet Muhammad recorded in one of the lesser-known Hadith, an Arabic word meaning "traditions."

However, Syeed says the Quran does indeed assure Muslims—men or women—who die while defending the truth of Islam that they will receive special rewards in heaven. Trigger words such as "virgins" are probably misinterpretations, with the promise actually implying "companions" or "loyal friends" for those who make extraordinary sacrifices defending the faith.

"The implication of sex in heaven is, of course, absurd—just as absurd as the idea of eating," he said. "In a divine setting, why would we need reproduction or need to metabolize food? Those concepts border on the ludicrous."

Syeed stresses that rewards for extreme sacrifice do not include suicide of any kind, which is strictly forbidden by the Quran. "There will certainly be no reward for blowing yourself or someone else up," he says.

But special rewards are promised, for example, for any Muslim who inadvertently dies fighting in *jihad* (a religious or holy war against infidels) against aggressors occupying one's homeland and trying to eradicate the Islamic faith, he notes.

"But it certainly does not mean material wealth and comforts, in earthly terms, and most certainly does not mean free sex in heaven—for men or women."

? ? ?

"**Why** don't Jehovah's Witnesses accept blood products, even if it means saving their or a family member's life?"

—TINA S., female

Readers Respond

"Out of respect for the sacredness of blood, we do not take blood transfusions, because God promised good health to us if we did. Yes, we might die, but we would die faithful to our God Jehovah and His Son Jesus Christ. Then there is a hope of resurrection and everlasting life. We're not willing to sacrifice our relationship with our God to live temporarily in this system of things."

—FAITHFUL WITNESS OF JEHOVAH

"It is really difficult to believe that people would let their children die because of superstitious beliefs. Freedom of religion is one thing; murder by neglect quite another."

—ED H., 56, white male

"Ed: Our beliefs are based on a book that has not changed since it was completed almost 2,000 years ago. What has changed is man's ideas on various subjects. Just 200 years ago, it was considered good medical practice to cut a small hole in a person's foot and let the 'extra blood' seep out. The Bible's view on blood clearly showed that this practice was wrong, but those who disagreed with blood-letting at the time were considered superstitious fools. Now it is the norm to pump foreign blood into the human body. Granted, this practice is more medically founded, but it is just as much against Biblical principles as the other. After all is said and done, a doctor cannot guarantee that a blood transfusion recipient will live any more than he can guarantee that one who refuses a transfusion will die. The only one who can guarantee life is Jehovah God. I will always choose over a man's way."

—M.A.M., 26, Jehov

Y?Check

First things first, says J.R. Brown, chief spokesman for Jehovah's Witnesses, headquartered in Brooklyn, New York: Witnesses aren't indifferent to life, irresponsible, or religious fanatics. They are simply following the directives in the Bible.

"We didn't invent it; it is God's law, dating back to Noah at the Ark and restated in Christian times," Brown says.

Biblical passages such as "Only flesh with its soul [its blood] you must not eat" (Genesis 9:3–4); "[You must] pour its blood out and cover it with dust" (Leviticus 17:13–14); and "Abstain from . . . fornication and from what is strangled and from blood" (Acts 15:19–21) are quoted liberally in Jehovah's Witness literature and at its official website, www.watchtower.org.

Although the verses are not stated in medical terms, Witnesses view them as ruling out transfusion of whole blood, blood components, and platelets. However, they aren't absolutely prohibited from using some components, such as albumin, immune globulins, and hemophiliac preparations, and must decide individually whether to accept these, Brown says.

"The problem is that people have read cases in the media or heard them on TV that sensationalized a case, where a doctor said 'this person died because they didn't accept a blood transfusion.' Yet more knowledgeable doctors have worked with bloodless approaches and wouldn't agree with that."

These bloodless therapies might require more skill on the part of a surgeon and more caution by doctors who might otherwise waste or spill blood "simply because they have five bags they can hang and use," Brown says.

Brown himself had triple bypass surgery at the "Bloodless Center" at Good Samaritan Hospital in Los Angeles, one of a number of such centers Witnesses have helped set up at various hospitals nationwide. Using techniques such as sucking up blood around incisions, cleaning it, and putting it right back into Brown, doctors avoided having to use blood transfusions, he says.

"Yet these things aren't publicized. I didn't have any headlines when I came back to New York."

Other common techniques include allowing a heart/lung machine to take over the function of the heart during surgery and, with large losses of blood, employing blood substitutes and "volume expanders," he notes.

For Witnesses who do accept blood transfusions, it is viewed as a sin—but it's not the end of the line for them as members of the faith.

"In a moment of weakness, you may see your life slipping away or feel pressure that you must use blood," Brown says. "In that case they need to repent, as anyone else who has committed a sin. They are then given spiritual help and shepherded back to full health in the faith . . . You don't cast someone away."

? ? ?

"I'm an astronomer and give planetarium shows with star legends from around the world that I've learned from books and other white astronomers. I've read that some Native American cultures view stories as physical property—and that telling them without permission would be stealing. Would I steal by using the stories?"

—JOANN B., 45, female, astronomer

Readers Respond

"Concerning the use of mythology in your presentations: I have done the same thing at Lawrence Berkeley Labs science center. I incorporated all the mythos into the discussion. It is easily done and makes for a very interesting discussion. I believe it sheds insight on how different peoples see themselves and their place in the universe. I enjoy the Arabic and Egyptian sky mythos. They both have a very deep spiritual 'sexiness' to them. Just incorporate a little of all of them into your discussion and you will astound and amaze your audience."

—JONATHAN D., 31, black male, astronomer

"There are many Native American astronomy stories that have been released for general use. However, if using the stories of a particular Native American Nation (i.e., a Seneca or other Iroquois story), it's a good idea to contact the tribal leaders to at least secure informal permission. Most tribes are flattered that other races (especially whites) are interested in hearing their stories."

—JOHN, 30, white with Cherokee ancestry, amateur astronomer

"I know how you can tell a few stories the right way: Let Native people tell them. The University of Michigan's Museum of Natural History has a planetarium show called 'Legends of the Three Fires,' and it is narrated by a well-known Native storyteller. I have seen the show, and it is done very well. The best advice I can give is that if you want to tell a story . . . get the people who tell the story best!"

—NICKOLE, 19, female, Cherokee, Blackfoot, and white

Y?Check

Gabriel Horn, a Native teacher and former cultural arts director of the Minneapolis American Indian Center, sees correct use of legends during such presentations as one measure of whether they've been misappropriated.

"An oral tradition usually didn't have ownership. Rarely do we see the poet's name at the end of a Pre-Columbian poem. I understood this to be an egocentric idea which the People did not encourage," explains Horn, who has written titles including *The Book of Ceremonies: A Native Way of Honoring and Living the Sacred* (New World Library, 2000). "I could acquire a song with permission from someone, but would not think of using that song without approval and without knowing its intent and meaning just because I liked it."

Written translations for non-Native audiences inevitably distort or lose some part of a story's meaning, but the fact that star stories were written down probably prevented some of them from being lost to the ages, Horn says. In retelling such stories, the astronomer should be respectful and should take Native connection to the stars seriously, Horn says. It's a rule that applies generally to relating other people's traditions.

"I have been outraged at some of the things I have seen and heard, stories about Trickster told by people who have no understanding what and who Trickster is and that such a being is intricately connected to so many Native American beliefs in one form or another. I have seen Native people quoted in beautiful books and non-Native editors who have made a significant amount of money taking these quotations and reprinting them, yet the sacrifices of those whose words they truly belonged go unmentioned and their people not compensated. I think something is wrong there."

At the same time, Horn says, Native Americans can't copyright every facet of their culture and keep it from others.

"Sometimes Indians, like any people, can be our own greatest enemy . . . by censoring knowledge in a dignified presentation and knowledge that is readily available in a library, we may deny our beauty and intelligence to a world that really needs it, though certainly you can understand why some Indians can be miffed."

? ? ?

"**Why** do some Hindu males engage in wife-burning? Is it done to a woman just because she gave you daughters instead of sons?"

—JOHN L.

R eaders Respond

"In most poorer, non-Western, highly agricultural societies, there is no such thing as retirement pensions or Social Security. Most people are extremely poor, and the only security in old age is their children. In many of these cultures, women have no rights. They exist to marry and have children. They cannot go to school, work decent jobs or own property. Economically, a baby boy is the top prize, while a girl is just an unnecessary drain on the family's resources. The cards are stacked even more against girls by simple physiology. Boys have higher mortality rates, which ups the ante considerably. Religion is usually part of the undergirding social structure and can contribute to the situation, but it's usually not the prime motivation."

—PETER P., Roman Catholic

"I am not sure exactly what this question is referring to: the Hindu 'custom' of sati, wherein a wife commits suicide (on his funeral pyre) when the husband dies, or some report of a wife being burned by an angry husband. If the latter, it is a deplorable case of wife abuse, a human-rights violation and murder. We shouldn't try to find cultural reasons or justifications for it, such as the response above. If the question is regarding sati, then it would be useful to realize that this practice has never been a universally accepted Hindu custom by any stretch. It is certainly condemned today by 99.9 percent of practicing Hindus."

—P.K.M., 29, Indian

Y ? C heck

According to Mangai Natarajan, associate professor at the John Jay College of Criminal Justice at City University of New York, "Bride burning," which has been known to occur in India if a groom or his family believe his new bride's dowry is too small, has nothing to do with Hinduism and happens among the country's Christians and Muslims as well.

Some research has indicated thousands of deaths—some by burning—are tied to dowry disputes, but it's hard to prove how many women have been hurt or killed, says Natarajan, who trained in India as a counselor for juvenile delinquents and women in distress.

Natarajan says that new brides worry that leaving an abusive husband will humiliate their families and make it harder for younger sisters to get married. And if a woman is burned to death, the fire can hide crime scene evidence and be mistaken for an accident.

Natarajan says burning is more common in towns with easy access to fuel and that in more remote communities, some wives die by poisoning or end up at the bottoms of wells.

Historically in India, some women also burned to death after their husbands died. That practice, called sati, was rooted in Hindu scripture and was supposed to be voluntary, but there were accounts that women were forcibly tied to funeral pyres. Sati was outlawed in 1829, when India was controlled by the British.

Laws passed after India's independence also prohibited sati, but occasional cases have continued into the twenty-first century. Temples in some areas have commemorated the practice, and there have been court battles over whether to allow prayers there.

? ? ?

"HOW do African Americans perceive God? Do they pray to a white God or a black God?"

—N. CARMAN, 17, white female

Readers Respond

"I view God as a spirit, neither black nor white; however, it does pose an interesting question. Man was made in God's image, and through the Bible we know that the Garden of Eden was smack in the middle of Africa. So does this make God black? Maybe, maybe not. Does it matter? Should it? Nope. I think we shouldn't lie about what we know, but we shouldn't sweat what we don't."

—DEMETRIS, 35, black male, Christian

"When I pray, I am not picturing a black or white God. No eye has seen Him, so I can't really say I can picture what He looks like. He is God. What does it matter what He looks like?"

—T. JONES, black female, Baptist

"God is as different in people's eyes as we are to each other, but isn't that the beauty of humanity? I asked my five-year-old daughter what God looks like, and I am a little sad to report He is an old man with a white beard, but she is, after all, only five. I still have hope that her paradigms will be shattered."

—JENNIFER, 31, white female, Christian

"If I had to choose a human form, God would be female and multiracial or black, since the first man is almost uniformly accepted to have originated in Africa. Jesus is another matter. I find it very difficult to accept Him as portrayed in most paintings as white. He is described in the Bible as having curly/woolly hair and as being Jewish. It seems unlikely he looked like the Eurocentric image we're used to seeing. And many of us know that Jews can be quite dark in complexion."

—LATONYA, 34, black female

"Why does God have to be any specific color? For all I care, The Universal Creator can be purple or any other color I am in the mood for. I am a Neo-Pagan and, therefore, my God takes on many forms: Male/Female, Wind/Water/Earth/Air, Animate/Inanimate. Mostly I find that the Higher Power I pray to looks like all people. After all, weren't we created in 'His' image?"

—DAWN M., 36, white female, Neo-Pagan

Y?Check

In some ways, blacks do see God differently from most whites, because He offers hope to change racial injustice, says James H. Cone, a theology professor at Union Theological Seminary in New York City and an African Methodist Episcopal minister. Historically, "the real question is how white people perceived God, because that always had an impact."

Whites, as America's most powerful ethnic group, could define God in a way that suited their purposes, he notes. In the plantation culture of the antebellum South, white ministers could argue that the Bible condoned slavery. Generations later, others could say it was right in God's eyes to preserve America as it had always been, which meant freezing out blacks from chances for success and influence.

Blacks, of course, wouldn't accept that God condoned such discrimination, and instead gradually saw Him as a source of liberation, personally and for the country. Cone says that Martin Luther King Jr. carried that idea of God into the civil rights struggles of the 1960s.

"He not only reinforced the perception in black people of God as a liberator, but he helped change white people's perception of God—to have a God who is truly liberating for all people," he says. And he goes on to propose that that sense, in turn, sparked the Black Power movement in American culture and affects African Americans' ideas still.

"It's going to continue as long as white supremacy continues. And white supremacy is, you know, pretty solid right now. White people run the world."

? ? ?

"AS a practicing witch, I would like to ask those of the Christian faith or other faiths why they assume we are devil worshipers."

—DAWN E., female, witch

Readers Respond

"If you are interested in invoking metaphysical power, we Catholics believe the only safe avenue is by calling on the power of God. We are prohibited from using any means of contacting 'the other side,' i.e., ouija boards, tarot cards, fortune-tellers, psychics, etc., mostly because we consider these sources the 'false prophets' we were warned to avoid by Christ. Most Christians question the source of the power you invoke. I understand that those who follow Wicca have a well-developed theology that explains the sources from which power is legitimately claimed. Most Christians would dispute the validity of that theology."

—SUSAN J., female, Catholic

"Unless someone is a religious fanatic, they can usually understand the basic tenets of another person's faith without necessarily agreeing with it. Respect for another's beliefs should be a two-way street. Don't get into some long, drawn-out religious argument with someone who vehemently wants to convince you that their religion (or their version of it) is the only one, true faith. Part of Wiccan teaching is that there are many paths, and that each person must find their own."

—WITCHWOMON, Dianic witch for the past 15 years

"In Christianity, if you are not 'for' God, you are against Him. This polarity of positive and negative is total, so if you worship, but you do not worship God, then you are worshipping the devil."

—J. BARNES, 25, Evangelical Christian

"Wiccans, as well as followers of other major religions, believe in the sanctity of life. We have our own tenets regarding harmful acts upon others, just as Christians have their Ten Commandments, including 'Thou Shalt Not Kill.' It seems ironic, then, particularly in the context of the Christian Ten Commandments, that so many human lives have been sacrificed throughout centuries of religious persecution and religion-based warfare. Even here in the United States, human blood is shed every day in the name of religion. And there are still those who see a pentagram and call it the 'devil's' work, when in reality, 'evil' lies in the refusal to accept another's beliefs and let them practice the religion of their choice without persecution. If there were a supremely evil being (which my Wiccan faith's tenets do not recognize), it would surely be having a good laugh at all of us."

—KRISTINA A., 34, female, Wiccan

For Linda Harvey, who founded the nonprofit organization Mission: America in 1995 to "give fellow Christians up-to-date information on issues like feminism, homosexuality and New Age influences," witchcraft is a form of rebellion against the Bible, which approaches faith by saying there is only one God.

"This rebellion takes the form of spiritual rebellion, not simply 'I will do something that is outside the bounds.' That is basic human rebellion. Christianity accounts for that through forgiveness and penitence," she says. "Spiritual rebellion is 'I will worship something that has no relationship to God the Father or Jesus,' and on a more practical basis it becomes a nature-based worship."

That traditionally means pagan worship, or the worship of fertility gods and goddesses, traditionally where people involved in witchcraft gravitate, Harvey says. And many of its practitioners might think they are worshipping something benign, she says.

"Witchcraft believes the source of spiritual power is a nature goddess. They may believe it is a nature god and goddess together; they may believe it is maiden, mother and crone, or their own power within and manifestation of a goddess," she said.

However, she says, sorcery is also a part of the belief system.

"Modern Wiccans call it casting spells, a procedure to contact or harness a spiritual power defiantly not the God of the Bible, to harness that power for the user's own wishes. There is no idea of submitting to God's will," she says. "What is key is [that] the practitioner wants to be in charge, that they want to harness this spiritual power for their own purposes."

In the end, "If you are not a believer in the Trinitarian God, you have thrown your spiritual destiny into the other camp," Harvey says. "And ultimately the guy in charge is Satan, the epitome of spiritual evil.

"The Christian model is that the more you openly try to make contact with a spiritual entity that is not Christ-centered, the more your own spiritual life goes away. You become increasingly in danger of being lost in space."

? ? ?

"Do Catholics consider oral sex a sin?"

—J.B., 20

Readers Respond

"I was confirmed in the Catholic Church at 13 but no longer practice. Oral sex was not often discussed in my church or school, but I never heard any mention of it being immoral by my parents. Although Catholics are widely reputed (rightly) as being against birth control officially, it is not necessarily true that all proper sex within a Catholic marriage must potentially lead to procreation. Oral sex, and sex during pregnancy, for instance, are permitted. Of course, many Catholics also practice birth control against the wishes of the Church. In my opinion, oral sex is sex and negates virginity, and I think the Catholic Church might (unofficially) agree with me on that point."

—JULIA R., 31, white female

"The Church teaches that sex is sacred and should be saved for a committed relationship, but the average person (including many Catholics) ignores the Church's ideals and just wants to know how far he/she can go without technically breaking any rules. It's this kind of silly thinking that leads many Catholics to think they can engage in *any* sexual activity short of vaginal intercourse and still remain 'virgins,' technically. This is what happens when people worry too much about the letter of the law and not about the ideals behind the law."

—ASTORIAN, 39, Catholic male

"When I was growing up Catholic, all forms of sodomy were considered sins. This includes oral and anal sex. I am not a Catholic now, and so I do not feel the same way as the Catholic Church."

—MIKE, 27, Christian white male

Y? Check

According to James Akin, senior apologist for El Cajon, California-based Catholic Answers Inc., the largest Catholic apologetics and evangelization organization in North America, the Church holds that oral or manual stimulation of the sexual organs is permissible "for arousal that leads to the marital act."

However, oral or manual stimulation deliberately leading to climax in a male, thereby preventing intercourse, would be deemed "gravely sinful," he says, which is especially clear when it is used as a way of frustrating the procreative side of sex.

Indeed, Pope Paul VI, in his 1968 encyclical letter *Humanae Vitae* (Latin: *On Human Life*), reemphasized the Church's condemnation of "any action which either before, at the moment of, or after sexual intercourse, is specifically intended to prevent procreation whether as an end or as a means." Similarly, the Catechism of the Catholic Church states: "Every action which, whether in anticipation of the conjugal act, or in its accomplishment, or in the development of its natural consequences, proposes, whether as an end or as a means, to render procreation impossible is intrinsically evil" (CCC2370).

Open to debate among some orthodox Catholic moral theologians, according to Akin, is whether oral stimulation that leads to orgasm in women is sinful, as a woman reaching climax would not prevent the marital act in the way a male climax would.

? ? ?

"When I tell Christians I'm an atheist, they often react as if I've revealed a horrible secret. Then it's common to be treated as if something were wrong with me. Why is this?"

—BRITT, 28, atheist

Readers Respond

"To a Christian, to deny our Creator is to deny the very basis by which we live our lives. We believe salvation and eternal life come only through believing in Him, and Christians are supposed to try to lead others to Christ. For this reason, it hurts me to hear someone say they are an atheist because they do not know the joy the Lord can bring to their lives, and it also worries me for them to not have eternal life through God's gift."

—ANN D., 27, Christian white female

"I am in a similar situation, but reversed. I am a Christian, and many of my friends are not. They tend to regard me strangely and make derogatory comments about Christianity. It's fear of what is different and unknown."

—LAURA H., 22, female, Christian

"A huge percentage of people in the United States (94 percent) believe in some kind of deity or supernatural force. Atheists are saying that all of the religions are entirely wrong and cannot be reconciled with reality through minor theological changes. That's why it is more disliked than even minority religions."

—SETH S., 18, atheist, raised Jewish

"I can't imagine looking at all the wonders around me and believing it all comes from and returns to nothing. To me, thinking I'm only here because some molecules happened to come together in the right format and that when I'm gone, I just disappear, is just plain egotistic and selfish (not to mention a rather hopeless arrangement)."

—CINDY, 42, white female, Christian

"I do not like to think of anyone, especially a friend, living without the positive influence God can have on their life. I believe a Christian should respond to you with great kindness, and use this information to share with you the joy they have found from their relationship with Jesus Christ. As for believing themselves to be better than you, I believe these people need to remember that Jesus taught to 'consider others better than yourselves' and had a great regard for those who kept themselves humble in the eye of the Lord. Please do not let the image of the few (and the rude) Christians you have encountered sour you on Christianity."

—DEBBIE L., 34, female, Christian

Y? Check

Many Christians can find legitimate reasons to feel sad that someone is an atheist, says Peter Kreeft, a philosophy professor at Boston College and author of the *Handbook of Christian Apologetics: Hundreds of Answers to Crucial Questions* (Intervarsity Press, 1994), among other books about Christianity's intellectual aspects.

"Christians are commanded to love all human beings, and they naturally pity those who do not know their Father," offers Kreeft. "A second reason is that they believe it is good for people to know truth, especially important truth, and they believe atheists are deprived of this great good."

But because the impulse to love others runs through other faiths, he says Christians probably aren't the only ones who'd feel pain at hearing an atheist's professions.

"God is the source of joy, and knowing Him is the greatest joy possible on Earth, so there is a third reason for pity," Kreeft adds. "Most people would react with pity if someone told them that they did not believe in love, or honesty, or trust, or beauty, or hope, since most people not only believe these things are true but they know that these beliefs also give them joy. So there is a natural pity. And since pity is rarely appreciated because it contains an implicit insult, there is a confusion and embarrassment about expressing it."

Beyond the spiritual fulfillment they find, Kreeft says, Christians who study their faith deeply also find belief in God absolutely rational and might not understand how an intelligent person could think otherwise. So what should they do about a person who disagrees? Kreeft's advice is to talk honestly and to sincerely ask an atheist to explain his beliefs. Beyond the intellectual reasons, there will be personal reasons, and a believer should ask about those, too.

? ? ?

"**Why** do some whites attempt to use aspects of Native American tribal religions, often through paying money for something? And when they do, why do they insist it's an attempt to 'honor' or 'join' us, when for the most part they don't live in or work for the benefit of our communities?"

—ANGELA P., 22, Mandan/Hidatsa/Cree female

Readers Respond

"Your question reinforces the axiom of 'You're damned if you do and damned if you don't.' Society demands that we explore and accept Native American and other cultures, but then when we try to do just that, we are criticized for doing it because we don't live in the community."

—STEVE J., 42, white male

"The problem is not that white people want to learn about us. It's that so many think of us as quaint holdovers. So some will do things that they would never do to other groups, like dress their kids up as 'Indians' on Halloween or have them do rain dances as Boy Scouts, or use insulting cartoons of us as sports mascots. Would they 'honor' Jewish people by having their own version of a bar mitzvah, or crowd out Jewish worshippers from the Wailing Wall so they could sell crystals?"

—A.C.C., Mexican and American Indian male

"I think some people are just bored with their own religion or have shallow religious views, so they partake in Native American culture because it is seen as hip and not a major conventional religion with structure. It's a lighthearted religious fantasy to them, a way to act spiritual without being spiritual."

—ROB S.

"When I visited a reservation a few years back, I felt great hostility toward whites. A restaurant I stopped at for lunch sold T-shirts reading 'WELCOME TO THE REZ. GO HOME, WHITE MAN!!' And I'm expected to approach Indians to learn more?"

—J.N., 27, white male

"I am a Pagan who uses learning tools from many different traditions, including yours. My primary interest there is in animal totems. I am not trying to join or honor you. I am not even trying to learn from you. I simply utilize some of the same tools in my own learning. I do know some New Agers who go about throwing money around to buy anything from dream-catchers to crystals to pre-prepared candles for rituals. I still haven't figured out what they are gaining from it, hopping from one tool to the next without serious study of any of them."

—S.B. GREENDANCE, 36, white female

"The Native culture holds huge mystique for the average American—so of course they want to buy it."

—BETH, white female

"At the center of this sort of impulse is something often referred to as 'white guilt.' Much of the rhetoric of multiculturalism, diversity, civil rights and so on does vilify white people, especially men. If we are innocent and proactive, we need not worry about whether someone will think we are racist, sexist, etc. If we are guilty, no amount of Native American trinkets, African art, Latin music, urban slang or Asian spirituality will exonerate us."

—BOB, 30, male, diversity educator

Y? Check

Some natives argue that their spiritual identity is being sold out. In March 2003, a group of spiritual leaders from the Sioux, Arapahoe, and Cheyenne even banned nonnative participation in some ceremonies, saying that participation and other reforms were matters of cultural survival.

To Stephen H. Buhner, a white herbalist whose book *One Spirit, Many Peoples: A Manifesto for Earth Spirituality* (Roberts Rinehart, 1997) deals with interfaith spirituality, sacredness should have no ethnic boundaries.

"Human beings often do not choose the kind of spirituality that reaches out and touches them," he says. "It is the Creator that initiates that touching, and we respond to it."

Buhner says he was called to Native traditions more than twenty years ago, when he took part in his first pipe ceremony under the guidance of a Crow medicine woman. While Native American religions don't seek converts, he notes that Judaism, Sikhism, and other nonproselytizing faiths accept outsiders drawn to their beliefs.

"I have never been able to understand classifying people or determining their capacity for sincere spirituality by reliance on their skin color," says Buhner. "Many Native Americans are Christian and blend their older ceremonies with their Christian devotions. Such blendings have always occurred—the human relationship with the sacred is a living dialogue."

In Cuba, New Mexico, the Walking Stick Foundation arranges retreats at which Native American and Jewish ceremonies are open to followers of each belief. The goal is to share wisdom, but there's a careful effort to preserve the separate religious identities.

"We sit in on each other's ceremonies and teachings, but we don't mix them," says Rabbi Gershon Winkler, the foundation's executive director. Winkler, author of *Magic of the Ordinary: Recovering the Shamanic in Judaism* (North Atlantic Books, 2003), says that Judaism and Native American beliefs have a series of similarities that owe to the aboriginal roots of both.

? ? ?

"A r e Jews buried in a standing position?"

—SCOTT, 39, white male, Christian

Readers Respond

"I've passed by several Jewish cemeteries in my neighborhood and have noticed that their gravestones are all right next to each other. It would support the rumor that they are buried standing up. All I know is that the stones are much too close to each other to allow room for horizontal burial. Maybe they cremate the bodies?"

—MARIAN, 20, Asian female

"I have never seen nor heard of such a thing. There is nothing I have read in the Torah or Talmud to encourage that type of burial, either. That is not to say it might not be practiced by some small faction of Jews (there are many branches of Judaism), but if it is, it is very rare indeed. The vast majority of Jews are buried on their backs."

—MATT, 21, Jewish male

"Jews aren't buried standing. Jewish burial customs are primarily meant to keep the process simple, dignified and equal. No matter how poor, wealthy, respected or disliked, all members of the community are supposed to receive the same funeral: a plain wooden coffin, a shroud and the same funeral prayers. There's also a voluntary group, called the Chevrah Kadisha ('Sacred Society') that cleans the body and guards it before burial to protect it from desecration."

—T., Jewish

"When I was a kid, a gentile asked me this very question. I could not fathom it. He answered his own question by saying that 'Jews were buried standing up so they could squeeze more bodies in the cemetery.' I took this to mean that horizontal burial took up too much space and more cemetery plots could be sold with a vertical burial. I was dumbfounded. I am unaware of vertical burial practice by Jews or any other religion anywhere. It is a crock. All are buried horizontally. Incidentally, in Israel, the Jewish dead are buried in a simple white cotton shroud, not in a coffin."

—MARK, 47, white male, Jewish

Y? Check

Anyone who buys into this myth is making, to put it one way, a grave error, says David Zinner of Columbia, Maryland, executive director of Kavod v'Nichum, an organization that works to preserve Jewish burial and mourning traditions.

"I remember there is one story somewhere of a person who asked to be buried upright with his cane in his hand so when the Messiah came he'd be ready to walk with Him."

"But, no," Jews are not buried in a standing position, says Zinner, who is also vice president of the Jewish Funeral Practices Committee of Greater Washington and responsible for the website www.jewish-funerals.org, a clearinghouse of information about Jewish burial traditions and customs.

Some of the basis for the question could lie in the closeness of headstones in older Jewish cemeteries.

"Older Jewish cemeteries didn't require liners," which are basically cement vaults, Zinner says.

As a result, "when you're burying just a casket, you can put them much closer together," he says. "You can put them literally next to each other." But the advent of large groundskeeping equipment brought a new problem—without support, the ground would sometimes cave in.

There are many other Jewish funeral customs and traditions primarily meant to be sure everything is simple and dignified, but the one Zinner gets asked about the most usually follows broadcasts of movies such as *Schindler's List,* in which Jewish families would place stones on graves they visited.

This was done as a sign of respect and to show the deceased is remembered, similar to placing flowers on a grave when visiting, he says.

? ? ?

"My questions are related to the veil, the burqa, all the trappings used in different parts of the Muslim world to cloak the female form. Are these not an insult to Muslim men? Implying that they're too weak to control their libidos and so the women have to do it for them?"

—EMMA, female

Readers Respond

"Ask the women why they wear the veil, and you will find that they are not forced to. Islam does not require them to cover their full face; a scarf to cover their hair is sufficient. Why aren't Christian nuns asked the same question? Western women think they are living in an equal society, but in reality they are the subjects of exploitation. We are not ashamed, because we have high regard for women. If you had something precious, would you not cover it for protection? The high rape cases in the Western world are evidence that men constantly subjected to erotic exposure lose their self-control."

—A. Khan, Asian male, Muslim

"How would you like it if all men thought about when they saw you was how your butt looked, or if they wanted to sleep with you? I'm veiled on my own accord. Let me put it this way: If somebody offered you a box of candy, and some of it was wrapped and branded and some wasn't, which would you choose? Most would choose the wrapped, because you know it's protected and sealed and hasn't been chewed by someone else. You'll be the only person to eat this candy, and it will give all its taste and enjoyment to you. Covered women are these wrapped candies, so not only do they give men who taste them by marrying them their best, they also take the best from them because these men trust them completely to have not been 'chewed or tasted' by someone else. By the way, I have a nice body and wear great, fashionable clothes. Sometimes people think being veiled means you have to wear a black cloth, which isn't true—I wear trousers and bright colors and everything."

—NOHA, 16, Muslim female

Y? Check

The purpose of the burqa is shrouded in misconceptions, says Sayyid Muhammad Syeed, secretary general of the Islamic Society of North America, a Plainfield, Indiana–based umbrella organization that has more than 300 affiliates across the United States and Canada.

He says that covering the flesh with a veil and cloak has nothing to do with helping men control their sexual urges. In fact, the burqa is only a cultural custom for some fundamentalist Muslims and was not prescribed by the Prophet Muhammad or the Quran, the Islamic Bible. Today the burqa reflects the traditions of very conservative societies, for example in Afghanistan, rather than the teaching of Islam.

He adds that ironically some women today may, therefore, be more restrictive in their dress than Muslim women were in the time of Muhammad.

The Quran suggests "decent, appropriate dress for unrelated people," both men and women. The emphasis on the burqa evolved during a period of Islamic empire-building in ultraconservative cultures— the garment resulted from powerful Islamic rulers who created "special rules" for their own families and subjects so various classes wouldn't mingle as readily.

"And somehow," Syeed says, "the idea behind the custom was misinterpreted to imply an Islamic injunction against the mixing of the sexes.

"This was really a dress code. Men, too, used to have something to cover their heads. And even today, men are mostly covered as well. But that dress code is very specific to certain regions."

He says the ideas of pure Islam and secular Arabic culture are often confused. For example, women in Saudi Arabia are forbidden from driving a car.

"Of course, Westerners think the ban on driving stems from Islamic law," Syeed says. "In truth, the Prophet [Muhammad] told Muslim men that we should train our women to be good camel drivers, and they became some of the best camel drivers. So we can only assume that today, the Prophet would be paving the way for Muslim women to become our best drivers."

? ? ?

"**Why** do Christian networks and shows feature people with really big hair and lots of makeup and gaudy, overdecorated sets? It makes me cringe, so I always skip over those channels."

—JENNA M., 28, Agnostic female

Readers Respond

"The styles you describe are prevalent in the South. That part of the country also produces the greatest number of 'Born-againers,' the people who watch these shows. I suspect the broadcasters are raising funds to perpetuate the TV show, with money left over to pay the evangelist. You are probably not the target audience in the first place."

—PAPPAJERRY, 66, white male

"Look who controls these networks and where the shows originate: CBN in particular—owned and operated by Pat Robertson straight out of the Bible Belt—where big hair and tons of makeup seem to never go out of style. They are targeting an audience (using very sophisticated marketing research) in order to garnish the most money possible. That target seems to be 'trailer park trash.' Then look at the Sunday morning fare on regular network TV—shows such as *Hour of Power* with Robert Schuller. This is from a mainstream church with modern, somewhat liberal beliefs. The high hair and tons of makeup are not there. Their target audience isn't selected for generating the big money, rather for getting the word of Christianity across to the masses. In so many words, CBN and their ilk are out to get money from an audience that studies have shown is most likely to send them money because they see some sort of 'kinship' with these broadcasters."

—MIKE, 42, Humanist gay male

"Saying that televangelism is a reflection of global Christianity—from tribal churches in Zambia to Western congregations—is like saying the entire world of music is shown on MTV. I, too, am appalled at the gaudiness. I see it as detrimental and over the top. I also take issue with a lot of the theology. A lot of it is off the wall and has nothing to do with the Bible."

—D., 21, Pentecostal male

Y?Check

Televangelists can be broken into three broad categories, according to Anson Shupe, a pioneer with the late Jeffrey Hadden in the study of religious broadcasting: There are "fixed-set" national programs, such as *Praise the Lord* with Paul and Jan Crouch of Trinity Broadcasting Network; crusaders, such as Benny Hinn, who take their message on the road; and minority or niche broadcasters, such as African American preacher Frederick Price.

It's the fixed-set televangelists who most often have the elaborate furnishings and showy outfits and makeup, says Shupe, a sociology professor at Indiana University who cowrote *Televangelism: Power and Politics on God's Frontier* (Henry Holt, 1988) with Hadden.

"These shows have become like Oprah or Letterman, with people coming on selling their book or hawking something, with a few songs thrown in," he says. "They've done their polls and market research, and they know what sells. Cable TV has allowed them to stay on the air . . . apparently enough people send in money for them to stay in business."

The big hair and ornate sets have a certain appeal to these televangelists' biggest audience segment: lower-middle-class, middle-aged females, he added.

"Jan Crouch is the new Tammy Faye Baker, with horrible makeup and a buffed-up hairdo like Dolly Parton," Shupe says. "But there's a sufficient-enough audience out there for that."

The bottom line is that these types of televangelists are normally preaching to the choir rather than making new converts, and to keep their core audience coming back for more, they have determined that a certain amount of entertainment and glitz is needed, he says. The formula apparently works: TBN is the world's largest Christian television network, featured on more than 5,000 television stations in the United States alone.

"I'm not doubting their sincerity, but you can see that there's a huge market out there . . . they are making fantastic amounts of money."

? ? ?

"What exactly are Mormon beliefs? Do the followers believe there's a planet Klobb?"

—RICHARD H., 19, white male

Readers Respond

"A few of the tenets from our 'Articles of Faith': We believe in God, the Eternal Father, and in His Son, Jesus Christ, and in the Holy Ghost. We believe that men will be punished for their own sins and not for Adam's transgression. We believe that through the Atonement of Christ, all mankind may be saved, by obedience to the laws and ordinances of the Gospel. We believe Christ will reign personally upon the earth. We believe in being honest, true, chaste, benevolent, virtuous and in doing good to all men. If there is anything virtuous, lovely or of good report or praiseworthy, we seek after these things."

—JASON E., 27, white male, Mormon

"Mormons believe that Kolob (not Klobb) is the name of the sun in the solar system where God's planet is located. One day on God's planet by Kolob's reckoning is a thousand days on earth."

—CAROL, 48, white female, Mormon

"I admit, we are a little different from other Christian churches . . ."

—NORM J., 23, white male, Mormon

"We do not believe in a planet 'Klobb.' We worship the namesake of our religion: Christ. If we worshipped some other being, his or her or its name would be in the title of the name of our Church. We believe that Christ was resurrected and that with His resurrected body, He lives somewhere, but where, I doubt anyone knows."

—EDWARD, 35, male, Mormon

Y?Check

Mormons believe God and Jesus appeared to Joseph Smith and told him the church as founded by Jesus Christ didn't exist anymore, says David Paulsen, a Mormon and a philosophy professor at Brigham Young University in Utah. Smith was also visited by other heavenly messengers, translated ancient writings into the Book of Mormon, and organized the church in Fayette, New York, in 1830.

"It serves as corroborating witness to biblical testimony that Jesus is the Christ . . . and the resurrected savior of the world," Paulsen says.

The Church of Jesus Christ of Latter-day Saints was so named by Smith in 1838. Original Christians were called saints, so logically, members of the Mormon Church are simply called latter-day saints, Paulsen notes. Mormon is a nickname given to them because they believe in the Book of Mormon.

Through further revelations to Smith from saints and apostles, Mormons believe God ushered in the biblically prophesied "times of restitution of all things" (Acts 3:21), when all things previously revealed would be "gathered together as one" in preparation for the second coming of Christ and establishment of the Kingdom of God on Earth, Paulsen says.

The Prophet Elijah appeared to Joseph in 1836, resolving a long-standing puzzle within Christendom, Paulsen notes.

"Christians have long wondered about the fate of those who die never hearing of or having a fair chance to accept Christ," he said. "God revealed . . . that by virtue of the sealing powers restored by Elijah, Latter-day Saints could perform by proxy for their deceased ancestors the sacred ordinances (including baptism and confirmation) required for entrance into God's Kingdom."

And what of polygamy and that planet?

Paulsen said plural marriage was revealed to Smith early on and first practiced in Utah when the saints were driven out of Illinois. But he said a subsequent holder of the prophetic office received a message that plural marriage had "done its job" and it was later prohibited by elders.

As far as Kolob, it's part of Mormons' beliefs, too.

Among the many truths restored to Smith was a correct understanding of the nature of the God and the Godhead, Paulsen says. Conventional creeds affirming that God "is without body, parts or passions" have long contradicted the Bible, which clearly portrays God and Christ as embodied persons. God and Christ told Smith that they are, indeed, humanlike in form and respond to prayers.

And "though they have not disclosed their location, they have revealed that the star closest to their throne is called Kolob," he says.

Still in Question

A Sampling of Religion-Related Questions
Seeking Answers at Y? (www.yforum.com)

"I would like to know the differences in the usage of Yiddish and Hebrew. Are the two languages related? Is Hebrew used for religious services and Yiddish spoken at home?"

—E.D.

"What do Pagans believe happens when people die?"

—ERIN S., agnostic

"How can anyone not believe in God? You can honestly look at yourself, knowing how complex your body is, and think you were just there from the beginning, or that some evolutionary phenomena happened?"

—ERIN, 20, black female, Baptist

"It seems like I know a very high percentage of single Catholic girls who are very promiscuous. I'm talking having two to three different partners each week. Does anyone else ever notice this?"

—SUSAN, 35, white female

"As an educated, rational and tolerant Jew, I have an irrational fear and hate of Christians (especially evangelists). Does any older Jew or Christian understand this?"

—NICHOLET, 15, Jewish female

"I'm an atheist and very much in love with a Muslim girl from Morocco. She doesn't think we should be together because of our different cultural and religious backgrounds. Her father does not approve of our relationship. Should I persist, or do people think it wouldn't work, anyway?"

—THIJS, 19, Atheist male

"How can the Ku Klux Klan and other white supremacists claim to be anti-Semitic if they worship a Jewish man named Jesus?"

—DAVID O., 31, Agnostic male

THREE

Potent Mix:

Men
and
Women

"**Do** women fart? If they do, you'd never know it from hanging around with them. When a woman is with her close gal pals and nobody is around, do they just let fly? Or when a woman is walking through the woods or something all alone, does she let it slide? I mean, I can't imagine anyone holding it in for their entire friggin' lives."

—ERNIE, 28, Hispanic male

Readers Respond

"Of course women fart. The main difference between men and women that I've noticed is that usually women hold them until they are away from other people. We can't figure out why men can't seem to do the same thing."

—LUCY, 26, Hispanic female

"I fart, and think it's funny almost as much as men do. But I wouldn't let *them* know that."

—LAUREN, 21, female

"Have you been living under a rock the last 28 years?"

—LASHAQUANDA, female

"I had a female friend several years ago who farted around me, and when I finally accidentally let one slide in her presence, she laughed at my apology and announced to a friend of ours: 'She finally farted in front of me!' For some reason, it is difficult for some women to admit to normal human functioning; we are unspokenly taught to hide things like farting and masturbation."

—S.R., 23, white female

"I just ate tuna salad with lots of onions, and I've been farting all afternoon. [Women] also burp, hiccup, pick various body parts and scratch ourselves. No, we don't do these things in front of other women very often, except maybe our sisters and moms and closest friends. We're taught that these normal body functions are unacceptable. The only man I feel comfortable farting in front of is my fiancé, which is no doubt a sign of true love and trust."

—RHIANNON, female

Y? Check

In a study published in the journal *Digestive Diseases and Sciences* in 1996, researchers led by Michael Levitt, a gastroenterologist and director of research at Minneapolis Veterans Affairs Medical Center, found no significant differences in the frequency of flatulence between men and women.

Levitt, who has studied flatulence for decades and is arguably the world's leading authority on the subject, found that of thirteen women and twelve men studied over a one-week period, the subjects, regardless of sex, emitted gas an average of ten times a day (give or take one emission).

An earlier study by Levitt found that although men tend to pass a higher volume of gas than women—about 120 cc (cubic centimeters) per passage to just 90 cc for women—women have a higher concentration of the dreaded hydrogen sulfide in their outbursts, which makes their odor intensity greater.

Ultimately, says University of Michigan professor Eric S. Rabkin, coauthor with Eugene M. Silverman, M.D., of *It's a Gas: A Study of Flatulence* (Xenos Books, 1991), what might account for the perception that women pass gas less frequently than men is that in some circles, flatulence is considered indelicate by women but more acceptable by men, so men might seem to pass more gas—whether they do or not.

???

"I cannot urinate in urinals or in front of other men. Is this a problem only I have?"

—PAUL, 25, white male

Readers Respond

"I, too, have trouble going in a urinal with other men present. I told my wife about this and she said it was homophobia, in that we are afraid other men present are checking us out. I know damn well the other men have no interest in what my penis looks like, but it still makes the hair on the back of my neck stand up. My wife says that women have no washroom hangups. As she puts it, 'You could be having a big, smelly poop in one stall and have a casual conversation with a woman in the other stall who is inserting a fresh tampon.' Go figure."

—MURRAY C., 31, white male

"I find for myself, it is the prospect of peeing on demand that causes the problem. When it occurs, it usually involves large lines in restrooms, no privacy and a self-imposed need to conclude my business quickly. All of these factors conspire against me, and as such I cannot readily pee."

—MATTHEW C., 40, white male

"I have the same problem and generally find myself sitting down in a cubicle automatically. I assume it just goes to show how insecure we are about our size."

—TOM, 22, male

Y? Check

People who find it difficult or impossible to urinate in front of others, either at home or in public facilities, suffer from a social anxiety disorder known as paruresis, or Shy Bladder Syndrome, says Steven Soifer, coauthor of *The Shy Bladder Syndrome: Your Step-by-Step Guide to Overcoming Paruresis* (New Harbinger Publications, 2001), regarded by many as the definitive look at the affliction.

It's difficult to say exactly how many people in the United States have full-blown Shy Bladder Syndrome, which for some can be an embarrassing and often life-disrupting disorder, according to Soifer, president of the Baltimore, Maryland–based International Paruresis Association and professor of social work at the University of Maryland.

In 1997, a social phobia subanalysis done at Harvard Medical School of the 1994 National Co-Morbidity Study indicated that 6.7 percent of a random sample of people in the United States had difficulty using a public toilet away from home. That would equate to about 17 million U.S. residents suffering from paruresis, although Soifer estimates only 10 percent of those, or 1.7 million, are so severely paruretic that it would constitute "a bona fide social phobia."

Among those seeking help from the International Paruresis Association, men outnumber women by a nine-to-one ratio, according to Soifer.

"Men are dealing with open situations in public restrooms, whereas women have private stalls," which tend to offer more privacy, he says.

Soifer goes on to explain that various treatments can be effective in reducing or eliminating paruresis. Graduated exposure, a desensitization technique that involves attempts to urinate in the presence of a "pee buddy"—someone with whom the sufferer is comfortable and familiar—can reduce stage fright, said Soifer, who holds workshops nationwide on such cognitive therapies.

Clinics that specialize in treating phobias and anxiety disorders can also be of help, as can medication, although Soifer cautions that antianxiety drugs should be used only "to get the person to the next level of graduated exposure."

He concludes that with time and effort, 80 percent of those suffering from Shy Bladder Syndrome get better using graduated exposure.

? ? ?

"**Why** is it that women universally want their husbands to be faithful? Isn't lifetime monogamy too heavy a burden on anyone, including women?"

—V.V., 40, French female

Readers Respond

"I would not do anything I thought might hurt or humiliate my wife. That's what is wrong with fooling around. As for a lifetime of monogamy with her, I consider it an honor."

—STEPHEN S., 31, happily married

"My (female) partner and I have been together eight years and have been nonmonogamous throughout that time. It has increased rather than decreased the trust, intimacy and stability of our relationship. Sex is not the most important part of our marriage; love and commitment are."

—SELENA, nonstraight female

"My wife and I both had extramarital affairs after promising to be faithful to each other. It has hurt us both. But through a lot of work and patience, we have regained each other's trust. Both of our affairs were caused by dishonesty. We learned before it was too late how much honesty and trust go hand-in-hand."

—MARK T., married 12 years

"I don't think it's only women who desire lifetime monogamy. Most men have a difficult time imagining the person they love with another

man. It requires time and energy to maintain an extramarital relationship, mistresses and spouses grow jealous of one another, and
each feels deprived of important time, or worse. It's just simpler to
stay with one person."

—D., white single female

"I'm a married woman who does not ask my husband to be monogamous (indeed, we both have other lovers). I do, however, ask him to
be honest and faithful to those agreements that we have made. Having sex with another woman is fine; not discussing it with me (among
other things) is not."

—CATHERINE, 25, bisexual female

"You're putting your significant other's life in jeopardy. AIDS is no
joke."

—DR. C.

Y? Check

Rutgers University anthropologist Helen Fisher studied divorce in
sixty-two societies and adultery in forty-two cultures for her ground-
breaking book *Anatomy of Love: The Natural History of Monogamy,
Adultery and Divorce* (W.W. Norton, 1992).

She argues that the best psychological data show that it is men,
not women, who depend more on having a single, faithful mate.

"Men suffer more when their mate dies," she says. "Men are
more likely to remarry if their mate dies. Husbands keep fewer social
connections outside the marriage. And it is men who get really jealous if they suspect their mate is cheating."

That stated, the idea that men and women are preoccupied with
such lifelong physical attachments is "an American myth," Fisher
says. "Men and women are entirely capable of having a strong at-
tachment to one partner while at the same time having a strong romantic desire for another."

She goes on to say that indeed, while 91 percent of the U.S. population is married by age forty-five, 50 percent of those end up re-marrying, with adultery the prime factor in marriage breakups. And it's not just men having the affairs, Fisher reports in *Anatomy of Love.* "Every time a heterosexual man is 'sleeping around,' he is cop-ulating with a woman. And since the vast majority of adults in almost all of the world's societies are married, logic upholds the proposition that when a married man is sneaking into the bushes . . . he is most likely copulating with a married woman."

In those instances when men and women do profess a desire for a partner who will be faithful, they do so for different reasons, Fisher's research shows. Men might desire a faithful mate to preserve their ego, but they also have more basic reasons that are tied to pre-serving their lineage: "They don't want to use their time and effort to raise a child that's not theirs," she says.

On the other hand, women who want husbands who don't stray desire it for psychological reasons, too, "but it's also Darwinian—to rear her young, she needed a faithful mate who would provide re-sources."

Fisher notes that in her multisocietal divorce research, a pattern emerged that if a woman already had enough resources, she was more likely to end her marriage.

For Davis Buss, a professor of psychology at the University of Texas who spent a decade studying mating behavior across cultures, how women react to a breach hinges on the type of infidelity in ques-tion.

For the acclaimed book *The Dangerous Passion: Why Jealousy Is as Necessary as Love and Sex* (Free Press, 2000), Buss's research team studied ten thousand people in thirty-seven countries across six con-tinents and found that women most valued *emotional* fidelity.

"Women key in on cues to a partner's feelings for other women," he notes. "A husband's one-night sexual stand is agonizing, of course, but most women want to know: 'Do you love her?' Most women find a singular lapse in fidelity without emotional involvement easier to forgive than the nightmare of another woman capturing her partner's tenderness, time and affection."

? ? ?

"**Why** do some men find breast implants so sexy? Many of the actresses on TV have malformed breasts that look like half of a basketball stuck to their chests."

—CHRISTINE, female

Readers Respond

"It's not the implants that are sexy, it's the size of the breast. To some men, size matters. It pushes their buttons, so to speak. To others, me among them, the implants are simply bizarre."

—DOUG, straight male

"It makes me sick to think this is what women are driven to by artificial standards of beauty. I think men who really like big breasts must miss something about being a baby or have some fixation on their mothers."

—CHRIS, 25, white male

"I am a 26-year-old male who finds large breasts extremely attractive. I cannot help at least glancing . . . However, recently I have noticed a lot more women my age and younger having breast implants, although their breasts are fine as is. I figure it must be a self-esteem problem. Would I want my mate to get a boob job? No way. Would I hold it against a potential mate if I found out she got a respectable breast enlargement? Maybe. I like large breasts to look at, but I prefer 'real' small to 'fake' big for other, important reasons."

—TARAN, 26, male

"I am also perplexed by guys who are into fake breasts. There's an attitude of 'of course they're fake, and I don't care!' To me, it's like a guy with a bad toupee. It looks ridiculous; it's nothing Mother Nature would ever bestow upon you, and you paid good money for it. What does that say about you as a person?"

—DIANE, 32, white female

"Some very flat-chested women could benefit from some breast augmentation. Then again, if you're talking Pamela Anderson warheads, forget it. Not so sexy."

—JOHN, 36, white male

"Visible breasts (cleavage or a tight blouse) do get my initial attention. However, after a few minutes of conversation on many such occasions, I have decided I was not interested in that woman. I am usually more a sucker for a woman's eyes and, yes, personality. I once knew a young woman who had a double-mastectomy and I found her to be very attractive and sexy."

—LAZARUS, 41, white male

Y? Check

America's infatuation with the boob job is expanding. After a survey of board-certified doctors, the American Society for Aesthetic Plastic Surgery reported the number of breast augmentations performed rose 147 percent between 1997 and 2002 to 249,641. Breast reduction increased even faster but was far less common, with a 2002 annual total of 125,614.

However, a man's appetite for a top-heavy woman is apparently not as insatiable as it's cracked up to be. In more than a decade of studies, psychologist Stacey T. Dunn at the University of Central Florida in Orlando has repeatedly found evidence that women overestimate men's desire for large breasts.

"We seem to be falling into this stereotypical trap," she says. "Men do prefer a size that is larger . . . However, it is not as large as women think."

Working with a scale that compares various breast sizes, she found that overall, men were most likely to pick a C-cup as the ideal breast size. That's larger than many women, and a lot of women's fashion is designed for B sizes. But when Dunn asked women what they thought men preferred, the answers were very different.

"The biggest. [Women] think that men all want Ds and up," she says.

Why men like larger breasts is an open question. Dunn speculates it might be partly biological. "Even though breast size has nothing to do with fertility, large breasts are very visible signs of femininity," she says.

? ? ?

"**Why** don't many women have motor skills? Most females can't throw a ball correctly or swing a golf club. When they drive, they hold the steering wheel in funny ways and are constantly trying to correct the wheel."

—ERIC, white male

Readers Respond

"Can you do fine needlework, swiftly julienne vegetables or build and wire a lamp? I can do two of these three things—which I believe require fine motor ability—better than most people I know. If I were a betting woman, I'd put down $5 that you wouldn't guess which two correctly."

—D.S., 32

"Women do have motor skills. I, for one, play a very good game of softball and can swing a golf club in the proper manner."

—KAT

"Girls are often told to 'keep your elbows to yourself,' 'keep your legs together' and 'take small, delicate steps.' The apparent lack of motor skills is lack of training and gender expectations."

—ADELE M.

"Motor skills will deteriorate when women are around men and get performance anxiety. For instance, my mother can't drive with my father in the car. She always thinks he's criticizing her."

—KATHY, 23

Y ? C heck

Doreen Kimura, a professor of psychology at Simon Fraser University in British Columbia who has studied differences between the sexes and biological influences on cognitive function for nearly forty years, says that women's overall motor skills aren't worse than men's, just different.

Kimura's research, summarized in *Sex and Cognition* (MIT Press, 1999), found that men on the whole are better at motor tasks that require spatial location ability, such as hitting a target with a dart or ball, and that they are especially at an advantage when the target is moving. Women, on the other hand, have more-developed "fine motor skills" calling for dexterity, such as picking up a washer and placing it over a metal rod, something that requires a series of manipulative movements.

Kimura says most researchers "interpret the differences between modern men and women as due to our long evolutionary history as hunter-gatherers."

Men, for example, would have been more likely to engage in long-distance travel and hunting for game, so their skills in spatial navigation and targeting would have become more developed with natural selection. In fact, studies of patients with brain damage suggest that certain control centers in the brain might enhance targeting ability in men and fine motor skills in women, according to Kimura.

Her research has also shown that there may be an "optimal level" of certain sex hormones, particularly testosterone, in the body that contribute to males' better performance at spatial tasks.

Although further study is needed, what does seem clear is that sports history and physique don't account for sex differences in motor skill ability; in fact, Kimura has found, there's a strong likelihood that the effects of sex hormones on brain organization occur so early in life that, from the start, the environment is acting on differently wired brains in girls and boys.

? ? ?

"What stops guys at nudist colonies and nude beaches from getting erections all the time?"

—RICK, white male

Readers Respond

"Most guys are too nervous to get an erection when they first go out to a nudist beach. Also, once we realize that courtesy requires we keep control, it's just a matter of concentrating on remaining calm. And just in case, most people keep a towel with them at all times."

—P.J., white male

"There is no off switch, nor is there an on switch. It does what it wants to."

—DAN, 23, Chicano male

"The reason men do not become sexually aroused is that they are exposed to the nudity on a regular basis. Men who do become aroused at the sight of a nude woman are probably under-sexed or over-sexed. In other words, not really mature sexually and not well-balanced enough mentally, physically or emotionally. There is a misconception that men are less capable of handling their sexual desires than women. Men want women to believe that, but it is not valid. It gives men an excuse when they've behaved badly."

—H., 35, white female

"I disagree that only immature males get an erection when looking at a woman. I have a penis and know that sometimes I get an erection for no damn good reason. Men do not have complete control, nor do we have the privilege that women possess of having subtle signals of sexual arousal."

—MARC J., 22, white male

"I frequent the nude beaches in California and have many friends who are nudists. We see nothing sexual about being nude. It's enjoying the sun, surf and sand au naturel. However, even among longtime nudists, the occasional erection does pop up for whatever reason. Any virile male will tell you erections can happen for no reason whatsoever (most males experience the common occurrence known as 'morning wood' in their sexually peak years of 15–35). If one finds oneself 'standing tall' on the beach, etiquette says to lie on one's stomach until the erection subsides, mostly out of consideration for the families with children who frequent nude beaches. On any nude beach you will get the occasional pervert walking around 'tall and proud' thinking he's going to get sex by flaunting his shortcomings. As these types tend to endanger the status of the beach remaining clothing-optional, they are told to take it elsewhere by the beach regulars."

—MICHAEL B., 41, gay white male

Y?Check

From sitcoms to *Playboy* cartoons, the idea that you can "spot the nudist having the most fun" has been hammered into the American psyche. But that's the last message nude recreation advocates want to send their textile-dependent neighbors, according to Gary Mussell, president of the Southern California Naturist Association.

Clothes-free clubs and resorts like to promote themselves as non-sexual, family-friendly venues that advocate accepting your body, warts and all.

"Think of a beach, only without clothes," says Mussell. "And then notice that the average age in this scene is about 45, in all shapes and sizes, with a definite under-representation of people between 12 and 30. You will see families and couples sitting on beach blankets or lawn chairs, quietly talking among themselves or peacefully sunning themselves.

"In other words, it looks like anyplace else in America where people might gather—all races, religions, occupations and philosophies—and the only thing all these people have in common is they like to do it without the encumbrance of clothes. . . . How could anyone unintentionally get an erection in such an environment? The answer is you can't . . . really!"

And the fact that everyone is in the buff might take some punch out of the picture, too. A quip that's made it into naturist cyberspace says that one nude reclined on a couch can be erotic, but 100 lined up for potato salad can't.

That said, "mistakes" do sometimes pop up, and Mussell says it's not a major problem as long as you don't prolong it, and stay far from children.

"Erections rarely last but a few minutes if unassisted, so just cover your affected area with a towel—or get into the pool or Jacuzzi—and remember, what goes up always goes down."

? ? ?

"**Is** it true that when women are together they talk in much more graphic, detailed and intimate terms about sex and their sexual partners than men do?"

—S.A., white male

Readers Respond

"I have no idea how men speak of sex when they're alone, so I can't compare. All I know is that I can discuss anything with my best girl-friend, and that includes sex. We don't give each other a play-by-play—mostly we ask questions like, 'Have you ever . . .?'"

—S., 20, white female

"I have asked my husband if his friends talk about sex, and he said never. But me and my [women] friends talk about sex in general terms, such as talking about going to a sex toy party, flavors of oil, how they tasted and things like that."

—DEBBIE K., 29, married female

"Women do talk openly about things such as sex with their female friends because of the comfort level there. Also, because society paints a more pristine picture of us and how we should 'behave,' we tend to share only with female friends the same things that men talk about more freely."

—D.L., female

"I disagree with D.L. that men talk about sex more freely. Teenage boys boast about their sexual exploits, whereas men will talk about casual sexual encounters. But in general, men do not discuss sexual matters pertaining to their [wives or] girlfriends."

—DAVE, black male

Y?Check

Hot-and-heavy banter among women is "probably a myth," says Lexington, Massachusetts, sex therapist Aline Zoldbrod, coauthor of *Sex Talk: Uncensored Exercises for Exploring What Really Turns You On* (New Harbinger, 2002).

Zoldbrod says she wishes more women—men, too—would discuss their sexuality more openly.

"Women won't really share their feelings about sex with others, or even about masturbation," she says. "I think men like to imagine women having all these intimate discussions about their sexual relationships, but women are as private as men."

Men, she says, probably like to imagine women sharing intimate details "because some men have such difficulty having a mature discussion on the subject.

"Let's face it," she says, "men will lie. They will brag. They will boast about what base they got to with a sexual partner, but there's little detail and no discussion of sensuality."

Zoldbrod acknowledged that women are "generally more verbal and communicative" than men, but they seem equally inhibited when discussing sexual partners or their own sexuality.

"There are exceptions in other cultures—in Australia and Europe, for example—where women are much more open in discussing eroticism and sex.

"Women enjoy a wider range of sexual activities and fantasies [than men]," she says. "They're more orgasmic. But they keep it to themselves for the most part. I mean, I'm a sexual therapist and a woman, and I have a hard enough time getting them to open up to me.

"A few years ago I was helping a friend who is a sex therapist do research for a book," she says. "I was collecting data for the book and passing out lots of questionnaires to women asking what they do sexually, what they enjoy, that kind of thing. It was all to be done completely anonymously. They wouldn't even respond when it was completely anonymous. So you can imagine how freely they talk with one another. Some of the women I asked to fill out the questionnaires were my close friends, so I asked them why they wouldn't respond and they just said it was way too private. So what does that tell you?"

? ? ?

"OK ladies: Does size really matter? My girlfriend says women tell men it doesn't only so they don't hurt men's egos."

—EARL, 37, white male

Readers Respond

"It depends on the size of the woman. If her vaginal canal is narrow and short, she could be satisfied by a small member. Her G-spot and cervix would be closer to her opening. If a woman's vaginal canal is deep and wide, then her partner's penis would preferably be longer and wider. If a woman's partner is just long enough and just wide enough for a perfect fit, tell her to keep him for life!"

—ERICA E., 24

"It can be so disappointing when a guy you really like has a small penis. I prefer 6 to 8 inches. Smaller is just not enough, and bigger leaves me sore and reluctant to participate."

—LISA C.

"A larger, skillfully used penis does enhance sexual satisfaction. But skillful, loving, oral and manual manipulation can compensate for a smaller penis size."

—V.B., divorced, black (mixed) female

"Yes! Yes! Yes! Size does matter. My first several partners were all around 5 or 6 inches, and don't get me wrong, sex was, um, nice. But when I met my husband (he's about 8½ inches), I had my first incredible, mind-blowing, G-spot orgasm. I also could achieve orgasm through intercourse, which until then I thought was possible only through clitoral stimulation."

—B. THOMAS, 21, female

"I have a friend who has an 18-inch penis in the rested state. I found myself following him around just because he attracted more women than he could handle. They all wanted a chance at him and would do almost anything to get to him."

—K.R., 51, straight black male

"To K.R.: An 18-inch (flaccid? really?) penis is not a turn-on for me. If I saw it, well, that would have to be one guy with a super personality to convince me not to run as fast as I could out the bedroom door. Ouch!"

—D., straight woman

"Sorry to tell you, but it is better to have the friction of being filled to the brim than to wonder if he is in yet."

—K.M.O., 39, white bisexual female

"A lot of times if we have to choose, we'll choose big."

—VICKY P., black female

"Short but with girth is fine, long and thin is OK, too. Short and thin—bad. Long and thick—bad."

—TORRI, 29, white female

"Hell yeah it matters! Any girl who tells you it doesn't is lying to herself and you. I prefer larger penises because there's more to work
with."

—ANGELINA, 23, female

"I prefer approximately five inches. Even at five inches, sometimes it
can be painful when inserted all the way."

—S. BAKER, 27, white female

Y?Check

A man's size might lead to a woman's sighs, but not always for the
reasons men think, says Jennifer Bass, spokeswoman for the
renowned Kinsey Institute for Research in Sex, Gender and Reproduction at Indiana University.

"It's much more of an issue for men than it is for women," she
says. "It's culturally important to some men."

Size generally isn't relevant in terms of a woman's satisfaction,
she says, because usually women don't depend solely on vaginal stimulation for orgasm. The size of a penis can affect whether a woman
finds a man exciting, but that's different for each woman—and, pre-
sumably, she's already found something appealing about him before
he's naked.

"A large penis might be arousing for some women . . . or it might
be frightening," Bass says.

Too much manhood can be too much of a good thing, she adds,
as some women find a large penis uncomfortable. But that's also an
individual matter.

"Women's bodies can accommodate lots of different sizes."

Still in Question

A Sampling of Male- and Female-Related Questions
Seeking Answers at Y? (www.yforum.com)

"Why are married men (not all, of course) with attractive and sexual wives choosing cyber-porn and sexual chat rooms over intimate sexual relationships with their wives? I'm struggling with this at home."

—Married 15 years, female

"Do women not read on the toilet? Men, do you read magazines and books while doing your duty? Please say yes—and let women know about the pleasure of a really good . . . read."

—J.M., white male

"Why are men so uninterested in marriage, while women can't wait?"

—JEN C., 21, white female student

"When a woman makes a comment about a guy's butt, what is she attracted to?"

—PETER, 33, Hispanic male

"I was wondering why some men with hair loss grow it long on one side and comb it over the top."

—KELLIE L., 25, female

"Do women enjoy anal sex, or do some simply tolerate it?"

—J.B., 30, white male

"Why aren't men more emotional, and why don't they let their hearts rule their minds?"

—KAVITA, female

"Do men think women aren't as genetically 'adapted' to excel in a technical field?"

—CHRISSY, 21, white female

"Why are most women unwilling to allow me to express any opinion about 'women's issues' in conversation? I am expected to silently 'listen and learn.' "

—TOM H., 36, white male

"My boyfriend of three months does not believe in foreplay. I love being caressed and romanced. The first time we had sex it was so awful and loveless that I cried (he doesn't know this). I am very much attracted to him. How do I tell him how I feel?"

—JAYNA, female

"If a woman refuses to have sex with a man because he has not provided a condom, is she considered a 'tease'? Shouldn't she expect him to have one?"

—APRYL P., black

"Why is it that every time you have a sincere interest in a woman, you have to be a jerk to get her attention?"

—ADAM

FOUR

Light-years Apart:

Age

"**Is** it unusual for a couple in their 60s to enjoy sex as much as my wife and I do? We love sex with each other, a little bi, and sometimes a little swinging."

—DON, 60, bisexual white male

Readers Respond

"Although I have found my husband and I have sex less often than when we were younger, it is still very enjoyable. My husband is several years older than I, and we stimulate and excite each other in different ways from when we were younger. It is gentler and more patient—with no distractions."

—PATTY, 61, white female

Y? Check

Younger people might be surprised to learn what's going on in the bedrooms of their elders, according to Joani Blank, a San Francisco sex educator and author of *Still Doing It* (Down There Press, 2000), a look at seniors aged sixty and older who detailed their sex lives to Blank through essays.

Blank, who's been involved for nearly thirty years in the field of sexology, says society has gotten the idea that a diminished sex life is inevitable with age, but that's not the case at all.

"It's not unusual to have sex over 60," says Blank, who added that her libido is still going strong at sixty-six. "We have such a notion about youth and that when you get older your sex life will decline, and then it's surprising (for an older person) when his sex life is good—and maybe getting better. That's the good news."

Data seem to hear her out that older people are still having a go of it:

- A 1999 study by American Association of Retired Persons, the national senior organization, found that of men surveyed, 8 out of 10 age 60–74 and nearly 6 out of 10 aged 75 or older currently had a sex partner, while of women, about half aged 60–74 and 2 out of 10 aged 75 or older currently had one.

- A 1999 "Sexual Activity Survey" done for the Association of Reproductive Health Professionals (ARHP) by Bruskin/Goldring reported that 62 percent of men aged 60–69 and half of men aged 70 or older were "very" or "somewhat" satisfied with their sex lives. The same ARHP study found that half of women aged 60–69 and 65 percent aged 70 or older were "very" or "somewhat" satisfied.

- A 1998 survey done for the National Council on Aging (NCOA) by Roper Starch Worldwide reported that 71 percent of men in their 60s, 57 percent in their 70s, and 27 percent in their 80s or older engaged in sexual activity at least once a month during the past year. The same NCOA study reported that 51 percent of women in their 60s, 30 percent in their 70s, and 18 percent in their 80s or older engaged in sexual activity at least once a month.

Based on her longtime research practice and observations, Blank says that the frequency and desire for sex—kinky or otherwise—among seniors is likely even higher than that found in the surveys.

"A lot of it is making your sex life lively when you're younger. It's the best insurance to having more sex when you're older," she notes. "It's an attitude adjustment . . . getting it in the brain in your 30s and 40s that you'll be sexual 'til the day you die. It's just like planning for retirement. You want to be sure you have enough money, well, be sure you have enough sex, too."

? ? ?

"HOW come it seems as though teenagers are afraid to take part in the care of AIDS patients?"

—SHANNON, 18

Readers Respond

"Many adults tend to shy away from taking care of AIDS patients, too. For one thing, there are many people who are still misinformed about the cause of AIDS and how it is spread. They could be afraid they will catch the disease just by being in the same room with someone else who has it. Also, working with many patients facing death can force the caretaker to do so as well. Many people, especially teenagers, are not prepared to do that. The preference is to maintain an illusion of immortality. Constantly being bombarded with the thought of death is difficult to handle."

—ADAOBI, 22

Y? Check

If anything, teens are potentially more open to learning about and confronting AIDS than other age groups, says Jennifer Kates, director of HIV/AIDS policy for the Kaiser Family Foundation in Washington, D.C.

"It doesn't appear teens have any more misconceptions" than adults about HIV, according to the foundation's national polling data, and in some cases they have less, such as in the smaller percentages of those aged eighteen to twenty-four who think the virus can be contracted by, say, sharing a drinking glass, she says.

This doesn't mean they don't worry about the disease, however: The foundation's National Survey of Teens on HIV/AIDS, conducted in 2000, found that six of ten want more information about how to protect themselves, more than half want to know where to get tested, and one in three are "very" concerned about HIV/AIDS. However, that doesn't translate directly to a fear of helping others: Kates says in her more than fifteen years of working and volunteering in AIDS advocacy, she's neither seen data supporting that conclusion nor witnessed it firsthand.

Kate Barnhart, case manager for The Neutral Zone, a New York drop-in center for homeless and at-risk lesbian/bisexual/gay/transgender youth, agrees. Now twenty-eight, she started an AIDS peer education team as a student at Stuyvesant High School in New York, helped open an AIDS resource center on her college campus, and ran summer peer education programs on AIDS and sexually transmitted diseases for the CASES program for troubled youth between 1994 and 2000. She's also coordinator of the youth committee for AIDS advocacy group ACT-UP in New York.

In speaking with thousands of teens as part of educational programs at high schools and colleges along the Northeast coast, Barnhart says the main reaction she has gotten is "How can I help?"

In general, misperceptions have subsided as knowledge and treatment have improved. In the past, teens encountering people with AIDS might be distressed to see their condition, which might involve extreme emaciation or Kaposi's Sarcoma lesions on the body, Barnhart says. But new antiviral medications can treat opportunistic infections when they occur, vastly improving patients' quality of life—primarily for those with access to proper health care.

"At first, people were dying, and there was a fear of getting close to someone and then losing them. That's a little bit less of an issue now."

? ? ?

"**Why** is it that older men seem to wear their pants higher on the hips than the rest of the population?"

—MIKE, 26

Readers Respond

"Forty or 50 years ago, trousers were made with more space between the belt and crotch; therefore, in order for them not to look baggy, you cinched your belt higher. Also, when a man gets older, most develop a 'spare tire' around their waist. I once knew a man who had his pants made especially to accommodate his large belly. His belt was above his belly and practically under his arms."

—JOSEPH L., male

"Many of us shrink as we get older. It's not the bottom half that shrinks (our legs don't get any shorter), but rather the top. As our spine loses moisture and osteoporosis causes the back to curve over, the distance from the waist to the head gets shorter. So when it appears that a man is wearing his pants higher and higher, what may really be happening is that his shoulders are moving lower and lower toward his waist."

—JUDITH G., female

Y? Check

As men age, what once were wide shoulders and a thin waist forming a V shape becomes more like a trunk, says Mark Evan Blackman, chair of the Department of Menswear at New York's Fashion Institute of Technology.

"All that area starts to fill in, and for a certain portion of the population they gain most of their weight in their bellies. Their backsides are flat, their thighs aren't that heavy, and so they have a choice: pull the belt up over the belly, higher, or wear it underneath the belly. So you've either got a 34-inch waist below, or a 40-inch waist above. It's a choice.

"A younger person is generally not going to wear his pants below or above their belly—they will still have enough muscle tone to wear their pants at the natural waistline," he says. "When you are older, your body has changed, but you have been in the habit of reaching at a certain height to button your pants. So if you gain 30 to 50 pounds, you are still in the habit of reaching to that place, whether it's now above or below the stomach, so that's where you'll wear your pants."

? ? ?

"**I** have a tongue piercing. In all other respects I look totally conventional. I am curious what your reaction would be if you saw it and me."

—ANNE, 19, female

Readers Respond

"The only thing that runs through my head is ow! Doesn't that hurt? I grew up in the San Francisco Bay Area, and it got to the point that if you *didn't* have multiple piercings and tattoos, people would look at you oddly."

—DOUG, 39, white male

"I would think you liked to have oral sex. Isn't that what tongue piercings are for?"

—AARON, 31, black male

"I would think there is some lucky dentist out there who is going to be driving a fancy sports car some day off your teeth. Not only do tongue piercings physically damage teeth, they make it nearly impossible to keep bacteria down. Hope you are keeping an eye on denture ads, because you will be wearing them."

—STEVE, 46, white male

"With the exception of ear piercings, I generally see piercings as a form of self-mutilation by people who are depressed, frustrated or have low self-esteem—although I accept that in some cases it's a purely artistic expression. Regarding tongue piercings, when I see a woman with one, it makes me suspect she's hornier or kinkier than average and perhaps not so innocent. This, combined with its subtlety, makes it the only piercing that I find attractive and acceptable."

—LEE, 26, white male

"My tongue is pierced, too. I don't think there is anything wrong with it, even though my mom was mad, but she got over it because I was living with my sister and she couldn't do anything about it. A lot of people think I got it because I want to give somebody oral sex. But I don't get down like that—I just think it looks cute on me."

—SIMONE P., 18, black female

Y?Check

Youths get piercings to send a message that they are rejecting mainstream culture—and that's exactly what mainstream culture thinks they're doing, says Victoria Pitts, sociology professor at the City University of New York's Queens College and author of *In the Flesh: The Cultural Politics of Body Modification* (Palgrave Macmillan, 2003).

"They are trying to express their individuality, but the irony is that . . . when we mark our bodies, we are doing something social, and about connectedness, because we are acknowledging how our bodies are social spaces that are read by others," says Pitts, who's interviewed dozens of body modifiers for her work.

"There's been an explosion of interest in the body across the whole culture," she says. "Makeovers and cosmetic surgery are less stigmatized, we're seeing newly invented health and fitness regimens, and medical technology is positioning the body as a frontier of exploration, with TV shows like *Extreme Makeover*. So it doesn't surprise me to see a rise in body art practice in youths."

People she's interviewed with body marks get them despite knowing very well that they are risky when it comes time to get a job or make an impression with those in positions of authority, she adds.

"A great example is this guy who had facial scarring and

stretched ear lobes like members of the Maasai Tribe in Africa, where the ears hang down. I mean, this guy is extreme-looking," she says. "He was traveling across the Canadian border and was held up for hours by the border patrol. They thought he was a psycho."

Even kids as young as twelve are finding ways around state regulations in order to get stuck in unique places, Pitts notes. However, vaginal and penile piercings remain the purview primarily of adults in the S&M, fetish, and alternative sex scenes.

Health panic about piercings to the contrary, they aren't that risky, with nerve damage unlikely because they are removable and generally not worn for long periods of time—kids move on to other interests after a while, she says.

As far as people with tongue piercings being more interested in oral sex, Pitts says that will go down as a myth as people become more accustomed to them.

"It's nonsense," she says. "Men in particular like to sexualize certain areas of the body, including the tongue. But there's no legitimacy to that argument."

? ? ?

"**Why** do old people talk so much? They just ramble, talking about nothing, and are as irritable as they want to be. To this day I don't call my great-grandmother because she talks too much."

—D., 28

Readers Respond

"Wait until you get old! My grandmother is 92, has a hearing aid and can only see out of one eye. She still does crosswords and sews, but mostly she sits around the house where she lives with my parents. She goes out one time a week to church. She's lonely and doesn't have a lot of things to do, so she likes to talk. She says her 'forgetter' works overtime, so I think the reason she tells me the same stories over and over is that they're the only ones she can remember at the moment.

I'm sure your great-grandmother is lonely, too. What's so important you can't call her for half an hour?"

—SUE

"If you can't understand that this is what old people do, you're a sorry excuse for a grandchild."

—GINA P., 36, white female

"I definitely don't want to be around elderly people who just keep rambling on and on about nothing, especially if I couldn't care less. I have better things to do than hear someone's mouth flapping."

—MONIQUE

"My husband's grandmother has Alzheimer's, and she's the only grandmother I've known since I was 14. She rarely connects words into sentences anymore, but last week, she was surrounded by the family who loves her. We sat and 'talked' with her for over two hours and had a wonderful time. As I talk with her, I cannot listen to the words, or my brain will go haywire. Instead, I listen to the tone and inflection of her voice. We had some great conversations, passing love back and forth in the form of sounds. That's what it's really all about. Listen for the love, and the stories will fascinate and enrich you. Don't give up on her."

—BETSY, 42, white female

Y?Check

Old people have lived a long time and might talk a lot simply because they want to share their many experiences, says David Solie, author of *How to Say It to Seniors* (Prentice Hall Press, 2004). They might even get cranky because they experience time in a different way than younger people and sense their impatience with them.

"They are on a different mission and use time in a completely different way than [younger people] do," says Solie, who talks to numerous elderly clients as CEO and medical director of Second Opinion, a Woodland Hills, California, insurance company. "Young people use time for *doing* things and getting a lot accomplished. The elderly use time for reviewing their entire lives in order to discover what's really important.

"This non-linear 'wandering' in old age may create rambling conversations, as well as the irritability of the great-grandmother in this example," he says. "So set a time limit with the great-grandmother if need be, then remind her when it's close to the end of that time.

"As for the 'rambling,' remember that older people often are reviewing their lives to find the meaning in their many experiences," he says. "Instead of tuning out or expressing impatience, we should focus on their conversation and show interest in their stories.

"By understanding their use of time and why they ramble on . . . we can transform our frustration with them—and their impatience with us—into meaningful conversation."

? ? ?

"**Why** are many elderly people afraid of teenagers? Do most of them think that just because some teens are bad that every teenager is a drug addict who doesn't care about anyone but themselves?"

—AZRAEL, 16, white female

Readers Respond

"I think it has to do with change and the realization by older people that they are physically getting weaker and cannot defend themselves the way they were able to in their prime. Some years ago, my parents were uncomfortable riding a subway late at night with a group of teens sporting colorful mohawks. The hairstyles and dress of the youths were totally unfamiliar to my parents, thus the discomfort. This unfamiliarity leads to much prejudice and bigotry in this world."

—NANCY, 45, female

"I think teenagers don't realize that they can be quite intimidating when they're in a group and older people have to pass them on the street. However nice they are individually, a group, especially of young men, can look quite menacing."

—SYLVIA, 62, white female

"I enjoy young people. I have several friends who are teens and young adults. I have not forgotten that I was once young and wanted to have fun. My friends are so tickled to have a 54-year-old who can relate. I consider myself a positive role model and mentor. I feel honored to have them as friends. I respect them—and they respect me."

—JO WILLIE, 54, female

Y? Check

With their piercings, spiky hair, makeup, and other accouterments, it's no wonder some teens can bewilder or even scare older folks, says Caroline E. Crocoll, program director for the Washington-based Generations United, the only national nonprofit focused on fostering intergenerational relations.

"In the past, when youths tried to distinguish themselves, it was still more in line with accepted norms," says Crocoll, a gerontologist and expert in family relations. "So there wasn't that fear. But the fact is we have a very violence-focused media. Everything in society seems focused on extremeness, in video games, sports, everything is to the nth degree of stimulation, and I think a lot of the older generation just doesn't understand it."

That can create a barrier to communicating with youths, leading to even more erroneous perceptions—particularly when news reports focus more on negative behaviors instead of the many good deeds youths perform in their communities, she notes.

Keeping the two age groups away from each other is not the answer, she adds.

"We've had a very intentional, planned effort at segregating older and younger people. They're working at different jobs and taking different paths, and they don't interact, so stereotypes develop," Crocoll says.

One remedy is for both young and old people to take part in intergenerational programs in their communities. Older people often provide the nurturing that youths need if they come from broken homes, and younger people can spark a sense of vitality and wonder in seniors, she says.

"We don't learn about what life is like in contemporary society by isolating ourselves . . . what's going to happen to a society that's afraid of each other, or not getting the benefit of the wisdom of an older person?"

? ? ?

"**Why** do so many senior citizens buy such large automobiles? I've observed many an older adult struggling to maneuver these large cars."

—R.J., 36, male

Readers Respond

"I think many seniors know that their reflexes are slower than they once were and drive larger cars because they provide more protection in case of an accident."

—DAN B., male, 26

"As a member of a senior family that has just purchased a minivan, I can tell you our reasons for wanting a larger vehicle: space-space-space, and comfort. When you are traveling on the interstates at 60 to 70 mph, you have a lot more confidence in a larger vehicle."

—A SENIOR CITIZEN

"Old people only appear to drive large cars. There are several phenomena at work: First, old people drive very slowly and, as hypothesized by Einstein and proved by Doppler in his seminal work *Aunt Tillie's Studebaker and the Reverse Doppler Effect*, slow-moving objects appear longer than fast-moving objects. For example, orbiting Space Shuttle astronauts reported difficulty distinguishing between the Great Wall of China and John Glenn's wife driving her Honda Civic. In addition, old people shrink, making the car look larger. It's not psychology. It's simple science."

—B. HALE, 43, male

"Kudos to B. Hale. Is there any other way to see it?"

—MIKE, 32, white

"My grandparents are in their mid- to late seventies and like to travel the country. They prefer traveling by automobile because they can stop to eat or use the restroom or whatever, whenever they prefer, as opposed to an airplane, where they cannot sightsee or do anything. They own a luxury SUV, and although I, the environmentalist in the family, have ribbed them about it being a gas guzzler, it actually makes some economical sense for them. When they travel from Texas to Florida, for example, they are almost always joined by two friends. So the SUV offers them enough space for the four of them plus luggage, and saves gas by taking one vehicle rather than two."

—JESSICA, 23, white female

Y?Check

Large cars are longer, heavier, and have larger doors than smaller cars, and they have lower floors when compared to SUVs—all things seniors like about them, says Xuehao Chu, senior researcher at the Center for Urban Transportation Research at the University of South Florida in Tampa.

But these behemoth vehicles cost more, have lower fuel efficiency, and are harder to drive, so why the preference for them among the older set?

Chu's 1994 report, "The Effects of Age on the Driving Habits of the Elderly," a study conducted for the U.S. Department of Transportation using data from its 1990 National Personal Transportation Study, remains one of the broadest investigations of the driving habits and car preferences of seniors.

In it, Chu found that of more than 20,000 U.S. households surveyed, seniors clearly preferred cars with a longer wheelbase—the distance between the front and back axles.

"The answer lies in the unique characteristics of some seniors," Chu says. "First, their likelihood of being involved in crashes is somewhat higher than that of the mid-aged, but their likelihood of being killed or seriously injured once involved in a crash is significantly higher than that of the mid-aged. Second, it gets harder for them to get in and out of a car because of physical impairment. It is even harder if the floors are high, as is the case with trucks and SUVs. Third, many seniors live in single-car households. Fourth, they do not drive as much as the mid-aged."

Ultimately, the benefits of a big car outweigh the costs in many older people's minds, Chu surmises, with convenience and safety the main selling points.

? ? ?

"**Recently** I discovered that my father, who is 50, is in a relationship with a 20-year-old girl. I'm trying to understand why I am so upset by this."

—FIONA, 25, Asian female

Readers Respond

"Try to get to know her before you make any final decisions on whether she's right for your dad. Everyone has the right to be happy, and your father is no exception."

—CHERYL, 52, white female

"Whenever I see a tremendous difference in age between a couple, I wonder what the driving force is in the relationship. For a healthy relationship to last, the people involved have to have similar ways of looking at the world. In your case, your father has lived a lifetime and a half longer than his girlfriend, so how similar can their outlooks be? I would be very worried about what is motivating them both."

—JACQUELINE C., 26, white female

"I am 25 and seeing a man who is 50. In my situation it is all about two like-minded people who fell deeply in love. However, I think you are completely justified to have your feelings. You need to talk to your father about it. I would approach him sympathetically and sincerely. I believe it is possible that it is genuine—though that is rare."

—DAWN, 25, female

"I had a relationship with an older woman and found the hostility of her children difficult to cope with. I couldn't treat them as kids (they were not much younger than I), and I couldn't treat them as siblings—I was sleeping with their mother. I suspect your mix of feelings is due to uncertainty over this woman's role (mother or sister)."

—IAN, 31, white male

"I am only 15 years younger than my boyfriend, so it's not the full generation difference you're describing, but he does have a daughter only a few years younger than I am. The only way you'll find out if the relationship is serious and equal is to keep talking to both of them. (In my situation, she seems to have prejudged me and consistently avoids us both.) I can understand why you're upset, but if you let that feeling damage your relationship, that I would call unjust—to all of you."

—L. MARCH, 30, white female

Y? Check

Vermont psychologist Philip Belove focuses on marriage and family in his workshops and writings and has been researching mid-life dating for the past five years. He had this to say about Fiona's decidedly mixed feelings:

"Don't be too hard on yourself. A lot of your reactions are because this situation is so far away from your expectations. It will of course feel like something is off here."

Managing the reactions first requires acknowledging discomfort, he says.

"You don't want to start pretending to not care about stuff you really do care about. Understand your feelings. Then try to manage them."

Some things he says to consider:

- Is this a case of not being what the daughter would want for herself as a twenty-something? Maybe she'd want a partner who was more equal in power in the relationship.

- Anyone would be suspicious of this relationship. Their difference in age is a big deal. They, too, know it.

- A lot of young women in Fiona's position would feel the relationship was vaguely incestuous. She must be wondering: What does this say about her own relationship with her father? How does he look at her? How does she even answer that question? So another reason for the upset is that it makes it hard to understand the relationship between the father and daughter.

- Ordinarily, we don't think about the sexual behaviors of our parents. Nor do we relate to them as one sexual being to another. This relationship challenges that notion.

- Is Dad being really self-indulgent? And if he is, then how to respond?

"In the end, you want to keep your loving connection with him, and that means recognizing him for who and what he is," Belove says. "And don't expect it to be all that easy. You will constantly have to be reflecting upon your instinctive reactions to him. Even that is a demand you might resent."

? ? ?

"**When** is it OK to correct an older person on something, especially when they are incorrect about a fact or history? For example, I have tried to speak politely to an elderly church member about a fact, but she told me to shut up and sit down somewhere."

—CHERYL B., 22, African American female

Readers Respond

"Diplomacy. Don't force the issue. If you know you are right, suggest they might be mistaken and correct them. If they are open-minded, they will stand corrected. If not, don't push the issue. If you know you are right, that is all that matters."

—KEN G., 36

"Older people enjoy feeling valued for their experience and wisdom. I would correct a much older person only if strictly necessary."

—A. MORGAN, 33

"Truth once was often established by power and authority, not by facts and reason. Some older people have a hard time turning loose of this. In all fairness, it is equally fatuous for a young person to assert that nothing of real value can be had from listening to the elderly and taking heed of tradition, the 'tried-and-true' ways."

—S., white

"I once heard my father relate information in Sunday school that I knew was incorrect. That evening, I called him from campus and told him I had been searching for that piece of information, but I could not find it. 'Would you please find it and tell me where it is, for future reference?' He readily agreed, because I was appealing to him as a Bible scholar, not someone in need of correction. A day or two later he called me back and said he had searched high and low and had not found it, either. I don't think he ever relayed that piece of information again."

—W. LOTUS, 29

Y? Check

When older adults speak, it's important to listen with "different ears," says David Solie, who interviews dozens of elderly clients every day in his role as CEO and medical director of Second Opinion, a Woodland Hills, California, insurance company.

"They are engaged in a process called 'life review' that we may not understand until we ourselves get old," says Solie, author of *How to Say It to Seniors* (Prentice Hall Press, 2004). "This compels seniors to sort through all the experiences they've had and shape them into something meaningful.

"This process can be daunting, sometimes causing seniors to get their facts 'wrong,' " he says. "However, getting it all right may not be as important to an older person and may well explain why the elderly church member in this case reacted as she did.

"She is not interested in having you verify facts; she is attempting to understand the most important pieces of her life and have you understand them, too."

We can help, Solie says, by listening carefully, especially when elders repeat stories and events. What's important is to understand the values in the stories and not necessarily the facts.

"Start by asking yourself what values these repeated stories contain: Courage? Faithfulness? Compassion? Forgiveness? By doing so we can begin to facilitate their life review and achieve better communication.

"After all," Solie says, "no one wants to be remembered for misstating a fact. We all want to be remembered for the values we embraced and shared with others."

? ? ?

"**Why** do kids feel they have to take their lives, and that they can't turn to anyone?"

—J, male

Readers Respond

"I'm a 14-year-old high school freshman and have been depressed for about 2½ years. I have attempted suicide once, but my parents came home and I was forced to stop. My plan was, and still is, to overdose on aspirin. Frankly, it is hard to explain the feelings associated with depression, especially in teenagers. Often, as in my case, you lose touch with reality. My friends tell me I have become 'too sensitive.' I alternate between crying and yelling, mainly because I do not know how else to express the pain I am carrying around inside of me. I feel like a hopeless recluse who can't do anything right. I think of suicide at least one time every hour of every day. Unfortunately, recognizing there is something wrong with me and knowing I need professional help is not enough to actually get it. It feels like I am at the bottom of a very dark pit and everyone else is living above me. The more I scream for help, the farther away they get. I sleep as much as possible on weekends, just to escape the horror that has become my life. I've lost any pretense of a social life. I am slowly wasting away, becoming a body without a soul. I am rapidly becoming more desperate, and my thoughts of suicide become more frequent and elaborate. The way I see it, the world would be better off without people like me contaminating the gene pool. Yet I am still afraid to ask for help. Afraid that my peers will see me as even more strange than they already think I am, afraid that I might be hospitalized and be forced to quit school for a few months, which would ruin my chances to go to a good college, if I haven't done that already. Perhaps, most of all, I am afraid that someone might actually listen."

—KATIE, 14, white female

"Dear Katie, why are you in distress? There is so much to life, of course life has its bad sides, but it also has its wonderful aspects, too. I do not know your pains and what you have gone through, but I do know that you are not in the worst position. There is so much to this beautiful and sacred world, it really has a lot to offer. Please try and seek help. Life is really sacred and should never be thrown away. You have so much to offer. If you think you have a rotten life, can you imagine how the hungry kids in Africa or Romania feel? Indulge yourself with positive things: flowers, candy, genuine laughter, good adventurous novels and good company. Please seek help. Take care and smile."

—IFY, 22, black female

"To Ify: Talk about devaluing someone's feelings! Should Katie feel better knowing she is only depressed and not starving or suffering some other fate? To her, her pain is just as real, just as devastating as anyone else's, and to say, 'Tut tut, come now, there are kids out there starving to death' sure does dismiss what it is she is feeling. It sounds like your heart is in the right place, Ify, but what anyone who feels despair to such depths needs is someone to really listen and care. Comparing their pain to someone else's does them no good and makes them feel insignificant."

—JAMMY D., 39, white female

"People commit suicide because they are suffering from an illness called depression, a chemical imbalance in the brain that is an actual illness just like diabetes or cancer. The only thing that will help is medication and therapy. You cannot 'will' this illness away by thinking how lucky you are to have what you do have."

—PEGGY, 39, white female, living with bipolar disorder

"Katie, this world needs more sensitive people. People who care are too rare in life. It is people like you who will try to reach out to other suffering people. The ones who have suffered are the only ones who can realize what other sufferers are going through. People like you are killing themselves every day to protect the world from themselves. In reality, the world is in need of more people like you."

—PRBECK, 52, white male

Note from the author: Help was found for Katie in her town after the proper agencies there were contacted.

Y? Check

Kids have suicidal thoughts for a number of reasons, according to psychotherapist Kathleen McCoy, author of several books on young people's physical and mental health, including *The Teenage Body Book* with Charles Wibbelsman (Perigee, 1999).

Among these: (1) They lack the experience to know that life goes on, even happily, after bad things happen; (2) They get stuck in "either/or" thinking ("Either this person loves me or I'm totally unlovable and doomed to a lifetime of loneliness"); (3) They feel un-accepted or even bullied by peers and fearful of rejection by those they love most; and (4) They tend to be impulsive and don't always realize the permanence of the "suicide solution."

"On top of this, substance abuse can lower their inhibitions to act on their suicidal feelings," McCoy says.

How can someone help a troubled youth?

"Don't minimize any problems they tell you," she says. "Listen and empathize. Broken romances, academic or sports setbacks, dis-appointments or rejections hurt at any age.

"You wouldn't say to an adult 'Oh, you'll get over it!' or 'It was just puppy love.' Don't say these kinds of things to a teenager.

"It is also important to express unconditional love, find a support group, get support from teachers or administrators, consider a change of school, and point out ways to survive and thrive despite a major loss or disappointment.

"Finally, emphasize that suicide is a permanent solution to what may turn out to be a temporary problem, and as long as there is life, there is hope," McCoy stresses. "Being there for the young person can do a lot to re-instill hope in his or her life."

Still in Question

A Sampling of Age-Related Questions
Seeking Answers at Y? (www.yforum.com)

"Why are kids feeling the need to join these bizarre cultures such as Gothic Kids?"

—DEB D.

"I always thought reaching the mid-40s was the kiss of death for women as far as dating. But I am noticing much younger men flirting with me. Do younger men really like older women?"

—VALERIE, 45, white female

"Why is it that people are required to have a license to drive and hunt, and you must be 18 to vote, but anyone may have a child? What do people think about passing a law that made reproducing a privilege, and what would be the impact?"

—JULIA S., 17, female

"Do parents of children 20 or younger realize how miserably they have failed in their duty to discipline and acculturate their children, and don't they realize they are creating a danger to society?"

—MARK S., 30, gay white male

"Do teenage girls feel pressured about how they should dress and what their bodies should look like because of models in magazines and on television?"

—KIMBERLEE, female

"What do you do if you're a kid and have no money?"

—JOSH, 11

"Everywhere we look, we see senior citizen discounts, for meals, hotel rooms and even in department stores. Do others, particularly seniors, think this practice should be discontinued?"

—K. ANDERSON, 42

"Is it wrong to have sexual desires at 13?"

—JOSH L.

FIVE

Up to a Challenge:

Disabilities

"**Why** do so many mentally disabled people have such poor-looking haircuts and 'nerdy' clothes? They stand out enough as it is without the clownish-looking clothes."

—PENNY, white female, teacher

Readers Respond

"Low-functioning children like those I've worked with (my teenagers had the intelligence equivalent of a two-year-old) are very rough on clothes. Many soil them, spill food and drink on them, etc., just as little children would. If you have to change them four times a day, what would the cost of clothing come to? If you don't like the way they look, befriend one and pay for their clothing and haircuts."

—JENI B., 33

"I worked with the developmentally disabled for more than three years. Even though the individuals I worked with were nonverbal, extremely developmentally disabled and did not have stylish haircuts or clothes, they touched my heart. Their emotions are often unconditional. I think we all could take a lesson from them. They don't look at clothes or hair or anything physical; they care just because."

—LEAH, 28, female

"As a kid, I spent a few years living in a mental hospital. Most of my clothes were hand-me-downs, and yes, they did look awkward. I was very aware of that, but there was nothing I could do about it. There was no one to go out and buy me nice clothing. It was very painful. Even today, when I earn my own money and buy my own clothes like everyone else, somewhere deep inside I am afraid that some of that 'clown-ness' stuck on me."

—SARA, 22, white female

"I am the parent of an 18-year-old boy with Down's syndrome. If he were left to his own devices, he would wear clothes until they fell off. In this regard, he is not much different from my 'normal' 16-year-old son. Both choose to look 'cool' by wearing baggy, ill-fitting clothes, but one looks worse than the other to me (I'll let you guess which one). I could insist on both wearing what I decree, but I am trying to adopt a hands-off approach to child-raising. Sometimes mentally disabled people are not much different from the rest of society, which chooses not to conform with other people's fashion expectations. I am proud of both of them because they are showing some initiative and individuality."

—IAN, white male

"While I'm not necessarily offended by your asking the question, please take the opportunity to examine why you asked, because, as a teacher, the values you model will be passed on to the people you teach."

—STACEE, 30, white female

This one's easy, says Margot C. Ware, a certified gerontological nurse in Canada who has worked with hundreds of long-term-care residents and specializes in helping set up homes for those with physical challenges.

"The reason we often see mentally challenged people in old clothes that are not exactly in fashion is financial," says Ware, who owns her own nursing agency. "Most of the mentally ill live in some sort of subsidized housing with nonfamily caregivers. The government provides an allowance for the person's care, which is not something anyone will get rich off of. So the simple truth is, most mentally ill patients have very limited funds available and consequently rely on donations and thrift stores for their wardrobe."

Not too many people throw away or donate Versace and Vera Wang, she adds.

"Similarly, many have their hair cut by the caregivers, who are often older couples, to save the expense of going to a salon, so the cuts often look like they were done with clippers and may have involved a bowl."

? ? ?

"I'm told paraplegic men still have the ability to father children. Is this true, and if so, how?"

—CARRIE, 22, white female

Readers Respond

"The man cannot actually have sexual intercourse, as he cannot have an erection. But semen can be extracted from the testes and used that way. Sorry if my answer seems crude, but this is the only way to say it."

—ZENIA, 19, white female

"It is possible to remove sperm either surgically or to induce an orgasm using an electric shock. Neither is pleasant, but being paraplegic, this doesn't really matter. Normal in vitro fertilization techniques can then be used to impregnate the woman."

—ANDY, 24, white male

Y ? C heck

Some men with spinal cord injuries can still have sexual relations, and for those who can't, there's still hope, says Dr. Mitchell Tepper, a leading U.S. expert on sexuality and disability issues. Tepper suffered a spinal cord injury at age twenty yet fathered a child with his wife, Cheryl, and detailed the methods they employed in the January 1997 issue of *New Mobility*.

Tepper goes on to say that only about 10 percent of men with complete spinal cord lesions ejaculate during intercourse, and that, along with decreased erectile function and sperm quality, adds up to high infertility rates among men with such injuries. Conceiving a child can be emotionally draining for both husband and wife and can take up to two years, but various methods of "Assisted Reproductive Technology" have met with success, says Tepper, who has researched the topic extensively at Yale and other universities, is founder of The Sexual Health Network and SexualHealth.com, and serves on the editorial board of the *Journal of Sexuality and Disability*.

"One assistive method, electrical stimulation, otherwise known as electroejaculation stimulation (EES), is usually performed under anesthesia in a hospital setting or clinic. An electric probe is inserted into the rectum to stimulate the nerves responsible for controlling emission and ejaculation," Tepper wrote for *New Mobility*.

On the other hand, vibratory stimulation—applying a vibrator to the penis—does not require anesthesia and can be done at home, according to Tepper, who used this technique with his wife. With the proper vibrator, this method can be successful at inducing ejaculation for more than 70 percent of men with spinal cord injuries.

? ? ?

"**Has** anyone ever cut themself before? And why? I have, because my mum accused me of stealing money from her."

—LOU, 13, white female

Readers Respond

"I've done it on and off for about 10 years. When someone hurts you, sometimes hurting yourself is acknowledging that you're as bad and useless as they say you are. You're confirming it to yourself, and that's not a good thing. I used to visualize my pain in that blood, and letting it out also let out the pain."

—SCARLET, 23, white female

"I'm a cutter—shoulders, arms, stomach, anywhere, really. I couldn't possibly talk to anyone about it, because that would mean my parents finding out, and I get so much pressure from them to be a certain way that they'd totally freak out if they found out."

—JESS, 14, white female

"About a year ago I began cutting myself on the palm of my hand. I did so for several reasons, the most basic being to prove to myself that I could withstand physical pain so the emotional pain I was in wouldn't matter. After several months of psychiatric treatment I'm all right, but I know a lot of people who aren't. If you continue cutting yourself, I cannot urge you enough to see a doctor, or if I can't persuade you of that, at least talk to someone you trust."

—ALEX, 18, Jewish male

"I cut just because I want to. It doesn't hurt and is a rush to some people. It doesn't mean you are deranged or have a screw loose or anything. Some people just believe in different things and like different things."

—RYAN, 18, white male

"I have been cutting myself for five years, and I did it because I felt like I was in control of something for once."

—TYESHIA, 17, black female

"When I was about 18, I used to cut myself on the insides of my arms all the time. I don't even remember why. I just remember feeling really sad and anxious and angry all the time. I would think sometimes about hitch-hiking really far out of town and just dying there. I had a tough couple of years, but eventually it ended. All the bad feelings gradually start draining away, and then I had some successes. I got some recognition at university, met some good people and things just started improving. Being a teenager is tough. You live a restricted, cramped life with rules you didn't choose or even agree to. Later, things get way better. You get some money, don't have to live somewhere you hate and, if you're lucky, find work you love. Hang in there."

—SUSIE, 34, female

Y?Check

Self-injury, particularly among pre-teens, is much more common than the public realizes, with a major onslaught of cases having begun in the past five to ten years, says Dr. Wendy Lader, clinical director of the eighteen-year-old S.A.F.E. Alternatives at Linden Oaks Hospital in Naperville, Illinois, the nation's first program designed to help those engaging in "repetitive self-harm behavior."

Lader argues that youths today are more disenfranchised, see less of their parents, receive less mentoring, isolate themselves at their computers and video games, and witness more uncensored sex and violence through the media than ever before.

"They are overloaded and have intense feeling states that they don't know how to manage. They see self-injury as an immediate way to cope," says Lader, who coauthored *Bodily Harm: The Breakthrough Healing Program for Self Injurers* (Hyperion, 1999) with S.A.F.E. founder Karen Conterio.

Cases of self-harm that Lader has seen include cutting with razors; scratching; rubbing the skin with erasers until raw and bleeding; burning oneself with cigarettes, chemicals, or gasoline; cutting off digits; breaking bones; hitting oneself with a hammer; bloodletting; and even self-injecting feces, urine, or the AIDS virus.

Lader and Conterio receive dozens of phone calls and e-mails daily from self-injurers, their friends, or their parents. When they make media appearances, they can receive thousands of messages in a matter of days.

"They self-injure as a way to advertise what they are thinking and feeling. I call it spicing up the cover so someone might read the book," Lader says.

Lader adds that parents would do well not to accept implausible excuses for very precise and repetitive wounds—and they ought not think that ignoring it will make it go away. In addition, eight out of ten self-injurers have an eating disorder, so parents should watch for the link between the two.

In addition, Lader advises that self-injurers should be professionally evaluated and taken to a trained therapist. They should be challenged to begin altering their thoughts of self-loathing, and to deal with their fears and anger directly, not through harming themselves. Those who argue that cutting is merely a form of self-expression fail to see that such actions aren't simply temporary youth rebellion.

"These are permanent marks that you can't grow out of. And if [young people] think they are communicating something, they will usually fail to do so. Most folks will just think they're crazy, which invalidates their emotional pain and the whole reason they are doing it."

? ? ?

"**How** do nonstutterers see stutterers? Do you pity them? Do you see them as regular people you could get to know? Do you regard them as less-intelligent? Is stuttering funny?"

—JEFF, 38, stutterer

Readers Respond

"I work with someone who stutters. I do see it as a bit annoying at times, even though I know he cannot help it. Often in my head I will be saying 'Just say the words, already, I am tired of waiting,' but I never actually say that and always patiently wait."

—D. MEERKAT, male

"My younger brother used to stutter a great deal, and of course as kids we picked on him, but we also picked on everyone else. His stutter wasn't all that big of a deal. I honestly thought my brother had developmental problems for the longest time because he stuttered, but I was wrong. His intelligence level is very high, and because of him I view all stutterers as regular folks—as I should have from the start."

—ANGEE, female

"I work in a technical support department for a software company and have spoken to several bad stutterers. I have confirmed this general view with the other techs in the department:

1) Immediately we want to laugh. It's like we are stuck in the punch line of a joke.

2) This feeling is quickly replaced with a sense of empathy because we know that the person we are speaking to is not stupid. We cannot imagine how frustrating it is to know what you want to say but fail to effectively communicate it.

3) After 5 minutes or so, the empathy is replaced by frustration at having to wait 3 to 5 times longer to do simple things because we are waiting for the stutterer to finish his sentence.

We all agree it is a sad condition and will try to ask only yes or no questions to speed things up. We do ask that the stutterer keep from 'making small talk' in the interest of time. It may seem rude in the end, but it is basically a time/impatience issue."

—JOSEPH

Y ? C heck

The average person views stuttering as negatively as mental illness, according to pilot data from an ongoing study shepherded by Kenneth O. St. Louis, cofounder of the International Fluency Association and an internationally recognized researcher on stuttering.

Stuttering, mental illness, and being overweight were given the biggest thumbs-down by individuals worldwide when they were asked how they would feel about possessing certain attributes, according to results from the International Project on Attitudes Toward Stuttering (IPATS).

"It tells me that stuttering is seen by the general public as a fairly serious condition," says St. Louis, a speech-language pathologist at West Virginia University and author of *Living with Stuttering: Stories, Basics, Resources, and Hope* (Populore, 2001).

St. Louis adds that stuttering needn't be the end of the world for someone, shouldn't be stigmatized and doesn't mean a person with the affliction is bad or incomplete.

"The predominant view of stutterers is that they are shy, nervous, quiet and nonassertive, but . . . if you interview stutterers, you will find an entire range of people, some who are outgoing, aggressive, some in between, some quiet."

In the IPATS study, people also expressed concern about their children having teachers or friends who stutter, as well as reservations about the extent to which people who stutter could get a job or work in jobs that require lots of talking. But many respondents also expressed a good degree of respect and concern for stutterers, with many saying they would wait patiently while a person was stuttering or that they would not feel particularly uncomfortable during one's stuttering.

"Overall, if stuttering could be viewed as just part of the normal human condition, then the stigma that motivates so many young people to go to incredible lengths to hide or disguise their stuttering would go away," St. Louis notes.

For example, he says, "A stutterer will tend to substitute synonyms for words they aren't able to say, becoming a walking thesaurus. Some are effective at it. Other youngsters never answer a question in class; they just shrug their shoulders. Or they'll order food they don't want because they can't order what they do want."

St. Louis concluded that in extreme cases, some people have even changed their names because they couldn't say their given name, or have moved because they couldn't say where they lived.

? ? ?

"I am curious about what people who have been blind from birth 'see' in their dreams."

—DAVID L., 13, male

Readers Respond

"I lost my eyesight when I was six months old, but for the most part, I don't remember it. Blind people see things in their mind just as anyone else does. It may not look the same as what 'seeing people' see, but I still see it—a tree, a car or myself. And when I dream, that is no exception. So the color red to you may be different than my color red, but it's red to me."

—JORDAN, 19, blind

"I am friends with a young woman who has been blind since birth. She tells me she feels sensations in her dreams, and that she is in situations in her dreams. As for color, she associates concepts with them. For instance, 'green' for her is a good thing because it is associated with a country she loves—Ireland. While she was growing up, her family helped her know what colors certain things are. She knows the grass is green and that the sky is usually blue because that is what she has been told. Color does not have the same meaning it holds for a sighted person, but she is aware of it."

—MAHALA, 19, white/Native American female

Y? Check

A number of studies related to the dreams of the blind conducted since the early twentieth century have reached four broad conclusions: (1) people who have been blind from birth dream as imaginatively as sighted people, but they lack visual images in their dreams; (2) people who become blind before the age of five seldom experience visual images in their dreams; (3) people who lose their sight between the ages of five and seven might or might not retain some visual imagery; and (4) most people who lose their vision after age seven have at least some visual imagery in their dreams, although it fades over time.

One of the most recent major studies to replicate these findings, by researchers from the University of Hartford, University of California, and University of Connecticut, drew on a sampling of 372 dreams from fifteen blind adults, who, over a two-month period, recorded their dream content on audio tape upon waking.

The study, the results of which were first published in the journal *Dreaming* in 1999, also found that the subjects in the study who were blind from birth used a very high percentage of taste, smell, and touch sensations to describe the imagery in their dreams: They "felt" the warmth of the sun, texture of a coat, or edge of a knife; "smelled" fire, tobacco, aftershave lotion, or fresh air; and "tasted" a cigar, cup of coffee, or an orange.

"The imagery and sensations in the dreams of the blind are generally continuous with the senses they use in their waking lives," the researchers noted. In addition, "The findings on those who lost sight at varying ages after early childhood suggest that visual imagery is gradually replaced by the sensations that come to be more important in their waking lives," the study found.

Other researchers, notably a team led by Nancy H. Kerr, also have found that blind subjects' awareness of events, places, or objects in their dreams does not depend on visual imagery, and that a lack of visual imagery does not "adversely affect the richness or narrative continuity of dreaming."

Kerr, whose 1982 report titled "The Structure of Laboratory Dream Reports in Blind and Sighted Subjects" first appeared in the *Journal of Nervous and Mental Disease,* makes the case for "a broader definition of dream imagery as mental imagery in order to eliminate the pervasive visual pictorial metaphor."

? ? ?

"When I worked in a small building with a limited number of restrooms, there was a debate about normally abled persons using the stalls that could accommodate wheelchairs. Some of us would use that stall if the others were full; some would wait until a regular stall was open, just in case someone in a wheelchair came in. How do wheelchair-bound individuals feel about this?"

—M., female

Readers Respond

"I used to be wheelchair-bound, but I think it is important to mention that not all disabled people who need a disabled toilet are in a wheelchair. I have never minded other people using disabled toilets, but then my bladder has always been fully controllable. However, a lot of disabled people don't have such good control. My mother has multiple sclerosis, and if she needs a toilet, she has to get there quickly! So I guess from that point of view, it's good for there to be a toilet reserved. Toilets are something we can all be desperate for, though, so it's not quite as bad as an able-bodied person taking a disabled parking space—that really makes me mad!"

—BETH

"I believe the intent of a handicapped stall is to extend accessibility, not impose exclusivity. In other words, first-come, first-served. If all regular stalls are full, I see no reason why one shouldn't use a handicapped stall. Someone in a wheelchair may have to wait a few minutes, but they'd have to wait if it were occupied by another wheelchair-user. Beth has every right to be mad about able-bodied people using handicapped parking spaces. I believe those who do should be thrashed to the point that they really do have need of that parking space."

—MARY

Y? Check

The federal Americans With Disabilities Act of 1990 requires all existing public restrooms to have a wheelchair-accessible stall in place when "readily achievable" by the facility, and that all new public restrooms have a wheelchair-accessible stall.

Brewster Thackeray, spokesman for the Washington, D.C.–based National Organization on Disability, which "promotes the full and equal participation of America's 54 million men, women and children with disabilities in all aspects of life," says that if there are long lines at a public restroom and no one who is disabled needs to use the handicapped stall, then "use it, but it is wrong to tie it up for an extremely long period of time, because someone who is disabled may come along and need it."

Using such a stall improperly, however, isn't the same as using a handicapped parking space illegally, he notes. "You can get towed away for using a parking space."

? ? ?

"I've always been curious about how sex feels to a blind or deaf person. Are there any different issues they face?"

—T. SULLIVAN

Readers Respond

"It 'feels' the same for us as it does for you . . ."

—JIM, deaf white male

"Being deaf myself and married for 30 years to a hearing person, I need only signal my partner with a touch and guide him to what I desire to have done. The same thing goes for him. If you are really in touch with your lover (hearing, deaf or blind), I think this is the same for all who are in touch with the one they love. And yes, sometimes the person doing most of the 'action' may have to look up and see or recognize what it is their partner needs. Don't we all? At least I think so. When we are fortunate enough to have an understanding person in our lives who will take the time to give us the ultimate pleasure, and we them, it doesn't matter what, if any, disabilities we have. This happens when you take the time to know the one you love, not only by body language, but by speech or simply touch."

—LINDSAY, deaf female

Y?Check

If one or more of your senses is minimized or absent, you can bet your other senses will likely be heightened, says Janice Epp, a clinical sexologist at the Institute for Advanced Study of Human Sexuality in San Francisco.

"Thus, a blind person may experience a keener sense of touch, taste, smell and sound. In terms of sexuality, this can translate to a very sensuous encounter leading to 'yummy' sex," she says.

"We can all learn something from this: not to place so much emphasis on the 'main event' that we miss out on all those wonderful sensations available to us."

? ? ?

"Our family was recently at the community pool. Our five-year-old son saw a little girl swimming who had lost her hand in some sort of accident. He was petrified when he saw it and ran under a towel for the rest of the time we were there. Now he's nervous about going back to the pool. What would be the best thing to say to him to make him less fearful of this girl and this type of situation in the future?"

—R.D., 39, female

Readers Respond

"Educate your son about different handicaps. I coached a 7- to 10-year-old softball team for girls last summer, and one of my all-star players had only one arm. Two years ago she had a tumor in her arm, and it had to be removed from the shoulder down. She was an excellent player, and I was proud to have her on my team. Children respond as they see other adults respond."

—TINA S.

"I spend lots of time teaching children about people with disabilities. They want to know, and they want to know now! Let your child know that all people have differences. If he gets a chance to see this girl again and becomes friends with her, you should allow him to ask questions. I always tell parents that children stare because they want to learn. Mommies and Daddies letting them hide away is not going to help the child or the other individual."

—M.C., female

Y? Check

What's striking about this particular situation is that the child reacted in such an extreme manner, says Paddy Rossbach, president of the Amputee Coalition of America (ACA), which represents people who have experienced amputation or were born with limb differences.

"Kids of kindergarten age are usually the most interested and the least critical or discriminatory of amputees," says Rossbach, who lost half a leg when she was run over by a truck at age six. "The thing that is always amazing to me is that a kid can go all the way up through the elementary grades, and then he gets to his early teens and the kids will start calling them 'tin legs' or 'bionic man' and really nasty things—even though they've been friends since kindergarten."

Rossbach goes on to say that such a strong, frightened reaction may point to myths or falsehoods a young child has heard or even been told by his parents. If this had been her child, she would have made sure to take him somewhere else, sit him down, and talk—and listen—to him to find out more about his fears. More than likely, he thought what had happened to the little girl might happen to him.

"He needs to be told that lots of people have things different about them, so he needn't be frightened about it," she says.

Stressing that an amputee is different—but not unhappy—is also important, says Rossbach, who has worked with child amputees for two decades.

"If you knew me a while you wouldn't even notice it," she says, adding that a parent can also point out an amputee's attributes. "They can say, 'Don't you think she's clever to do that, to tie a lace with one hand, or peel an orange?' "

As a side note, Rossbach stresses the difference between someone achieving passive acceptance of an amputee and those who are "amputee devotees" and "amputee wanna-bes"—people either infatuated with amputees or obsessed with becoming amputees themselves. Entire fields of psychological study have cropped up around such phenomena, which can even involve individuals cutting or shooting off their own limbs to accomplish their goals.

To help children learn more about amputees, Rossbach says the ACA has created a special curriculum called Limb Loss Education and Awareness Program (LLEAP) that can be taught in schools. Children learn about the social stigma of children with disabilities, particularly those with a limb difference, and are taught to recognize and appreciate differences in themselves and others.

? ? ?

"Is it alarming to be suddenly tapped on the shoulder if you're deaf?"

—A.S., 34

Readers Respond

"I became deaf when I was 21. I tend to startle very easily when people catch me unaware, especially if I am busy with something or concentrating. My wife, who has been deaf from an early age, and my son, deaf from an early age, do not seem to startle as often or as severely as me. But yes, it probably happens more often than for hearing people. That is also one reason deaf people try not to 'sneak' up on each other. I teach and ask students to flash the office light before coming in to avoid this startle tendency. No, the flashing light does not usually startle, because it is a customary warning."

—J.D. WEBER, 49, deaf male

"I have been deaf since birth, so I am quite used to people coming up behind me and tapping gently on my shoulder. However, if people make a sudden, loud noise (loud noises usually vibrate loudly), then I will jump, startled. Another way I can be startled is when people tap my shoulder in an uncomfortable, impolite way, such as in a quick, urgent way. Just be sure to tap shoulders in a gentle, polite way—then we won't be startled."

—E. HENRY, deaf white female

Y? Check

You can effectively communicate with deaf or hard-of-hearing people using various methods, but it's not a one-size-fits-all situation, experts say. Some people read lips, but others don't, and there are different levels of skill.

Tapping a person on the shoulder typically isn't alarming and is recommended by some as a practical way to get a person's attention at the outset. (Waving your hand is another option.) Rather than bluffing your way through, it's okay to ask advice from the deaf person.

"Ask the person what mode of communication they are comfortable with," advises Shane Feldman, a staff member at the National Association of the Deaf in Silver Spring, Maryland. "Most of the time, follow your intuition and adjust your communication mode if the deaf person feels uncomfortable with what you are doing."

In San Antonio, Texas, the city's disability access office produced an etiquette handbook cited as a primer by organizations dealing with disability issues. Here are some of its pointers: If you're talking to a person who lip-reads, make your facial expressions easy to see. That can mean facing into the sun (saving your conversation partner from contending with glare) or keeping hands, cigarettes, and other obstructions away from your mouth. A trimmed mustache will be easier to look past than one that's bushy and hangs over your lip. Shouting can make things worse on two counts: It can distort sound for people who use hearing aids, and it distorts your mouth for people who read lips.

? ? ?

"I'm an attractive, successful woman who uses a wheelchair. I am capable of love and intimacy and want very much to share my life with someone. However, men are afraid of or intimidated by me. Do you guys really think you would be looked at as pathetic if you dated me? Do you think a woman in a wheelchair is unable to have sex?"

—MARIA C., 31, white female, uses wheelchair

Readers Respond

"Yes, men are afraid of women in wheelchairs. And yes, we do think that maybe they aren't capable of having sex. You have to admit that is a possibility. And it's hard to bring up that kind of question, even after a few dates."

—MARK A., 32, white male

"Take the first step yourself. That will make it much easier for the man. And show your female beauty. Sometimes I have the impression many disabled people don't care much about their outer appearance. For example, I've never seen a wheelchair driver in a short skirt. Be courageous, self-confident and sexy, and your only problem will be which dinner invitation to accept."

—P., 20, white male

"Some people might fear being considered 'sick' for being attracted to a disabled person. Or that they'd be accused of offering out of sympathy. It all becomes easier to just look elsewhere for a date."

—KARL, 44, white male

"I am dating a woman in a wheelchair, and we have a great relationship. She is very able to have great sex. So to all those people in wheelchairs who are afraid they won't find anyone or that no one will want them, never fear. You will find someone. And to those who avoid people in chairs, shame on you. You might as well avoid people of different heights or colors."

—MICHAEL, 27, white male

"Both my legs were amputated six years ago. Men have been kind to me since I lost my legs and have even flirted with me, but they never ask me out on anything more than a buddy-type date. I look the same as before, and my personality is the same. The only difference is I now have no legs and use a wheelchair. I am quite capable of having sex. I used to hear myself referred to as a babe, but now I hear 'that handicapped/crippled/amputee woman in a wheelchair.' That said, I know women and men who found love after becoming disabled. Maybe having this body weeds out the men who really wouldn't want me, anyway. If we do find a lover, we will know they don't mind that we have less-than-perfect bodies. Good luck—to us."

—ANNE, female, amputee

Y? Check

Erica Levy Klein, author of *Enabling Romance: A Guide to Love, Sex and Relationships for the Disabled* (No Limits Communications, 2001) says that a common barrier that people in wheelchairs must overcome is the assumptions other people make about what they want and can offer in a relationship.

Klein, who's not handicapped, got her introduction to the challenges facing disabled people while dating her former husband, co-author Ken Kroll.

"It's a tough gig. . . . I would not have believed the stuff that disabled people have to put up with," she says.

Klein offers some advice: First, recognize that most men won't initially understand the abilities or problems of a woman in a wheelchair, but some have the potential to learn. A key step is to spot those men and begin enlightening them in a friendly, low-key way.

Because people's personalities are oriented toward either sights, sounds, or feelings, she cautions that those who are highly visual may have a harder time getting past the appearance of a disability.

"If you listen between the lines, you can tell in about 5 or 10 minutes what their sensibility is," she says.

Klein argues that it's important to pursue relationships energetically. Besides talking to men and asking girlfriends for referrals, a woman might run two sets of personal ads at the same time, one saying she has a disability and the other not, and think about whether to use a dating service targeting disabled people.

"You need to do a lot of different things at the same time," Klein says. "It can be very energy-draining, but it's worthwhile."

Dating challenges for wheelchair users aren't limited to women, of course. At www.icanonline.net, a website about disability issues, George Butera has authored dozens of pieces offering relationship advice for his "Guy's Point of View" column. A number of them include observations about how Butera addresses his paralysis in his romantic life.

? ? ?

"The achievements of disabled children rarely amount to much, so would it really matter if they received a substandard education?"

—K., 22, white female, educator

Readers Respond

"My brother was in a car accident in high school that left him in a coma. The doctors told us he would never come out of it, and if he did he would be a vegetable. They wanted us to pull the plug, but we refused. He finally came out of the coma six months later, on Christmas Day 1988, and was left quadriplegic. He had to be in a nursing home for quite some time, but from there he went back and finished high school in regular and special ed classes. His graduation was one of the proudest days of my life. Today he can talk and walk (with a walker). So all the money spent on special ed is not wasted. And this is only one example. There are so many others."

—BOBBIE JO, 28, white female

"I have a sight problem that isn't that serious, but I know people with much more severe disabilities than mine. Everyday life is challenging for them, so of course they won't achieve what 'normal' people would. When they do achieve something, though, they are incredibly proud, even if it seems a simple task to others. To achieve something often means you overcome something that is difficult, whether you are disabled or not. Different people achieve different things, and it means different things to the individuals. Don't push disabled people aside. They have a lot to offer."

—GLEN, 19, white male, partially sighted

"As a disabled person (I have been in a wheelchair since age six), I am appalled by such a suggestion. We are as entitled to an education as the next person, and we can learn as well or better than them in spite of our physical limitations. I hold a Ph.D. in molecular biology—not an easy task even for so-called 'normal' people. Everyone is entitled to an education, no matter what their situation in life. Would it be fair to limit access to an education only to those from middle- to upper-class areas—since statistically those from the lower social-economic areas are more likely to end up as criminals or on drugs? Wouldn't that be a waste of our resources as well?"

—D.D., 26, white male, paralyzed

"It is sad that in today's society, where all strive for perfection, there is little room for those considered 'imperfect.' I for one am glad that in the United States all that money is being poured into those disadvantaged mentally and physically. I wish the same were happening here in Kenya. All are the same in the eyes of God, and we cannot measure success in terms of achievements only. Success is in the process of trying and the strength one gets out of it."

—WANJIRU, 28, African female, social worker

Y? Check

There's a vast difference between limited potential and limited opportunity, says Dr. William A. Lybarger, who during the past thirty years has been administrator of a community hospital, provided professional supervision over a nursing home, and managed a community mental retardation program.

"A part of our American way of life . . . is that every person should have the opportunity to be all that they can be, to maximize their potential," says Lybarger, who teaches at Friends University in Wichita, Kansas, and is an expert witness in cases involving developmental disabilities, psychiatric facilities, community mental health centers, and special education.

"The fact that someone has some limit on their cognitive ability should not limit their ability to maximize that potential."

One of the things Dr. Lybarger has learned through his career is that "the reality in our culture is that we tend to devalue people who are different, particularly those who are negatively different. Sometimes we put people in a category or box, and once in that box it's difficult to come out," Lybarger says.

Lybarger adds that although part of this is necessary in life—from deciding whether we should get on an elevator with a stranger to whether we should trust someone—it serves us very well most of the time. But in some circumstances, we tend to unfairly "place" people.

? ? ?

"I have been fat all my life and am currently a size 26. I have had many unpleasant comments about my weight—kids teasing me when I was in school, and even as an adult, men calling out 'fat bitch' at me in the street and making vomit noises. I would like to hear how people genuinely feel about fat people and their appearance—and I don't want politically correct and 'nice' replies."

—JENNY, 37, white female

Readers Respond

"I think my true feelings for grossly overweight people are total disgust at what I consider a lack of respect. I know there are people who have weight issues beyond their control, but when I see people gorging themselves or blocking the entire aisle at a store as they drag themselves along breathlessly, or sitting next to me on an airplane with their bodies and limbs spilling over into my seat and pressing me against the fuselage, my reaction is that they have no respect for others, the limited resources on this planet or their own health and well-being."

—T.C., 35, white male

"I do not understand how, barring medical conditions, one can get up to such a high weight or how anyone can fail to at least lose some of it with a modicum of effort. Nor do I buy into stories of anxiety eating. Eating is a cause of emotional problems, not just a symptom."

—ALEX

"Just last week I saw a grossly obese man at a pizza place dousing his small side salad with three cups (cups!) of ranch dressing. It's tough to find sympathy for someone who eats with such willful disregard for his health."

—BRAD, white male

"It takes a minimum of discipline and effort to stay in reasonable shape, and if someone can't take care of themselves, I would have to question if they would be able to take care of their other responsibilities."

—KEN, 20, Asian male

"I am fat and that is just too bad for everyone else. Why do people feel like someone else's size is any of their damn business, anyway? Is anyone so perfect that they are in a position to judge? I may be fat, but at least I am not a mean-spirited know-it-all."

—EVIL, 28, white female

"When I was 11, I was larger than most girls, and the boys in my neighborhood were horrible to me. As I grew up, around 15 or 16, I began to slim down, and can you believe those same jerks who teased me without mercy actually wanted to date me? I kindly reminded them that despite my change on the outside, I was the same little girl who was hurt from their words on the inside. Then I told them to go to hell."

—ANJELA, 35, mixed race, female

"What annoys me about people who are overweight is how much they seem to hate themselves. I feel like saying: 'Why can't you just love yourself? It's your body, you put all that food into it on purpose, this is what you wanted, so be happy about it.' In short, I'm much happier with fat people who are happy about their fat."

—BELLA, 31, Afro-Caribbean female

Y?Check

"Fat bias" runs deep among the public, says Julie Ridl, author of "The Skinny Daily Post" at www.skinnydaily.com. Ridl has seen life from both sides of the scale. After being morbidly obese for quite some time, she dropped 100 pounds to "pass for thin" and now writes fitness and weight loss columns for those trying to slim down. Her site draws thousands of visits and attention from health and fitness writers from the *New York Times, The Washington Post, Time,* and others.

"I hear some pretty terrible things now, and experienced them then," she says. "Finding out what people think isn't hard at all."

Research shows that preferences for thinness run deep, Ridl notes.

"The biases are well-known: Fat people are thought of as lazy, stupid, out of control, somewhat debauched, jolly, generous, clingy, gullible [and] lacking in initiative, creativity and gumption," she says. "There are plenty of people who will tell you that if they'd have to choose, they'd choose some physical disability for their child over fatness, because of what it does to a person socially over their lifetimes."

As important as the biases that exist, Ridl believes, is how much they are reinforced within society.

"White women receive more fat bias than white men. Black women receive it, but less so than other groups. Why? Different societies feel somewhat differently about fat. I suspect white people spend more time pointing and laughing and expressing disgust over fat people within their homes among themselves, and this reinforces the idea that fat people are fair game. It's helpful to have obvious losers around, I suppose."

A self-described tough, independent woman, Ridl says she didn't feel overly affected by fat bias when she was obese, but she knew it was there.

"What I feel now that I pass for thin is the difference. Much more eye contact. Much more inclusion in group conversations. Much more socializing in passing on the street, in grocery stores," she says.

"I suppose I wasn't aware of how people would look away before. But I've become aware now that they don't."

Still in Question

A Sampling of Disability-Related Questions
Seeking Answers at Y? (www.yforum.com)

"When in a group, do deaf people whisper? Surely there are things discussed among deaf people that are not aired publicly."

—JOHN

"Why are people who are able to walk for miles inside of a shopping center selfish enough to apply for and receive a disabled parking permit?"

—LES H.

"How do obese men and women clean their backside after having a bowel movement?"

—MONICA A., 23, white female

"Why can't an alcoholic stop drinking? My brother is killing himself. I don't think I can watch much more of it."

—BOOZER

"I work in a small shop. We have an occasional customer who is profoundly deaf. His speech is very difficult to understand, so we usually communicate with notes. He can lip read pretty well. Is it impolite to augment my responses with sign language (which I know very little)?"

—M. PEACOCK, 32

"Why do people with Down's syndrome all look the same?"

—ASHLEY L., 14, female

"I tend to think I should automatically help a person with a disability, but I don't want to be a pain if the person does not want my help. Can anyone with a disability share his or her opinion?"

—SUZANNE F., 21, white female

SIX

Out of Place:

Cultural Divides

"**I**'m a Southerner and would like to know why it seems a higher percentage of people from New Jersey are rude."

—KRISTEN, female

Readers Respond

"I have lived in New Jersey for 20 years and have never really found my neighbors, friends or co-workers to be particularly rude. I think you might be mistaking our fast-paced lifestyle and need to get things done quickly as hostility. I was fortunate enough to view the difference between life in the North and the South when I spent my first year of college in Virginia. I found that although people were extremely friendly (yes, more friendly than in New Jersey), everything—including service in restaurants, traffic and just people in general—was horribly slow."

—NIC, 22, female

"As a native of New Jersey, let me first ask if you are confusing 'rudeness' with 'abruptness.' I will admit that with our more hectic pace of life, we can be abrupt. But perception is everything. I tend to see

Southerners as 'rude' because they do not allow for differences in people (religious, sexual orientation, etc.). If you were to live in New Jersey or anywhere in the metro area, I think you would find some of us very pleasant, and some very rude—just like anywhere else in the country."

—ANDY B.

Y?C heck

"People in New Jersey don't have much tolerance for rubbish," says David Lippman, a Newark, New Jersey–based historian and writer. "Especially in the northern part of the state near New York, they live in a high-stress environment, with limited amounts of time, in a densely populated area. This area and New York City—it's just a very different place to live."

That doesn't necessarily mean they're rude. Just, well, busy. And direct. To the point. Got it?

"For example, a visitor might find that people here have loud conversations right in the street," Lippman says. "A sister might yell at her brother, 'Ma says you gotta get in here, she's mad at you!' They're more open about what they say and think. They don't have time to waste." Lippman adds that many people develop their impression of "Joisey" via trips on the turnpike from Washington to Boston, or Philadelphia to New York, where they see all sorts of industry and oil refineries and equate that rough-around-the-edges feel with its residents.

Residents' legendary directness, though, is real—but it applies in good times *and* bad, he notes. During the 9/11 terrorist attacks, folks rushed to give blood, help at Ground Zero, anything to lend a hand.

It's getting people to look past generalizations about gruff New Jerseyites that keeps Suzanne Clare busy. As executive director of the Gateway Tourism Council in the northeast corner of the state, she works to promote the region.

"It's true, at least in this part of the state, everyone's doing five things at once. Why? We don't know. We just have no time, so we cut to the chase," Clare says with a laugh. "I hear jokes about New Jersey, but I also hear people say how very nice it us up here. Hey, we're a very nice state! Come see us!"

? ? ?

"My brother-in-law says people from Arab countries wipe their behinds with their bare hands. Is it true?"

—MARY M., white female

Readers Respond

"I spent some time in Senegal, a predominantly Muslim country. There, most people use their left hand along with water to clean themselves after going to the bathroom. Toilet paper is a rare find in rural areas. As to whether this is common in all Muslim countries, I do not know."

—G. SMITH, 40, male

"Only in Western countries is it usual to use toilet tissue. Asian countries (including, I guess, the Middle East) mostly use water. This ensures a thorough cleaning—eliminating the 'klingons' and 'widgets' that plague Western behinds."

—IAN, 32, white male

"Not only Arabs, but most Muslims, wipe their behinds with their hands. They believe it is cleaner as long as there is plenty of water and soap available. Would it be better to use toilet paper but leave some behind that has not been completely wiped off?"

—KEMAL

"I have lived in Egypt all my life, and I know no one uses their left hand for wiping off. The part about using water is truer: Most people here use both toilet paper and water."

—KARIM O., 21, Arab male

Y ? C heck

Paul Spinrad, author of *The Re/Search Guide to Bodily Fluids* (Re/Search Publications, 1994), felt it so important to get to the bottom of this one that he tackled it near the beginning of his cult classic about culture, bodily functions, and excreta.

Wiping with the left hand and then cleansing the hand with water or even clods of earth is popular in the Arab world and India, Spinrad reports, especially in rural areas.

"Many times they may also use wool or stones or whatever," he says, noting that use of the left hand stems from the practice of eating with the right hand. Many cultures in the Arab world and beyond, thus, find it insulting to eat or pass food with the left hand.

The majority of people in these same cultures still consider the Western world's use of toilet paper "completely disgusting," he says.

"They will even carry water around, in a little ceremonial water container, an ornamental thing, to use to clean their hand afterward . . . can paper really cleanse? No, you need water."

Paper produced specifically for wiping didn't come into vogue until the late nineteenth and early twentieth centuries in England, Spinrad reports in his book. Up until then, everything from corncobs and the Sears Catalog (America) to unspun hemp (France) to coconut husks (Hawaii) to sponges on a stick (Ancient Rome) sufficed for the job.

And we would all do well to become more comfortable with our bodily functions, anyway—and not be so skittish about scatology, Spinrad notes.

"We need to get rid of the taboos. Shit is an interesting thing. We should study and understand its psychological influence."

? ? ?

"I used to go out with a Scot who wore nothing under his kilt and insisted that this was the normal practice. Is this indeed so?"

—PAMELA B., 42, white female

Readers Respond

"The term 'true Scot' is used to describe a Scotsman who wears nothing under his kilt. In one Scottish regiment, there used to be a mirror on the floor of the regimental office, and any soldier suspected of not upholding the regimental tradition was ordered to step onto the mirror. However, I noticed an example of the problems involved when I saw a group of dancers-cum-buskers in a Glasgow street, and you could see that at least one had nothing under his kilt. I was not particularly bothered, but it could embarrass some people. Most Scotsmen wear the kilt only occasionally, and when they do I suspect that a significant number wear underpants, either because of embarrassment or the risk of accidents."

—CAMPBELL M., 41, white male

"As a bagpiper, I've had more than enough experience around guys in kilts during windy days when the age-old question answers itself. Yes, quite a few who don the kilt do so au naturel. Those who do this generally are older than those who wear underwear under their kilts. For those interested, there is a right way to sit down in a kilt so as not to show the world your ass(ets). Sit down with your knees spread wide so that the kilt is held down between your legs by the sporran (the purse worn in front of the kilt for just this purpose). Anyone who doesn't sit initially with their legs apart will eventually find them drifting in that direction anyway, only without sufficient slack in the front of the kilt for it to automatically hang down. When this happens, the world gets a clear view of one's personal preference of whether to wear anything under the kilt."

—SHELLY, 28, white female

Y ? Check

On any given day, whether it's at a Highland Games event in the United States or a wedding in Edinburgh, chances are the men wearing kilts have something on underneath, says Sally Nicol, whose The Scotland Yard Ltd. in Shelbyville, Kentucky, has been making and selling kilts and other Scottish goods nationwide for more than eighteen years.

"The common practice nowadays is to wear boxers under the kilt," says Nicol, who traces her origins to the Clan MacRae and Clan Campbell in Scotland.

The earliest record of kilts being used in the Scottish Highlands is about 1560. According to Nicol, before the advent of underwear, it was the norm for men in the Scottish military to let things breathe, so to speak, under their tartan cloth. That's not the case in modern times.

"Once in a while at a Highland Games, some show-off will say 'I don't have anything on' for shock value. You smile and say good for you . . . But most people do wear something under their kilt."

Practically speaking, Nicol notes, people competing in Scottish athletics need to wear boxers or briefs, or their body movements will expose more than their legs.

As a matter of fact, she says, the chances are slim of even seeing someone in Scotland today wearing a Plaid, as the tradition has fallen out of favor and is viewed as just a little hokey.

? ? ?

"**Why** are older Chinese males so obsessed with superstitious cures for impotence that they have depleted the world population of tigers, rhinoceros, bears and some forms of marine life?"

—JOHN, 44, white male

Readers Respond

"Your question begs a bigger question: Why do human beings everywhere feel their needs (medical, dietary, personal or otherwise) supersede the needs of the environment and other species? I think the answer is ignorance and/or lack of concern. Why would you eat meat knowing that acres and acres of rain forests have to be cleared for cattle to graze? Why would you eat meat knowing that animal wastes pollute our waters? Why would you eat another sentient being? Some people don't know the consequences of their choices, or they do, but just don't care."

—CINDY, 26, Asian

"If you followed environmental politics, you'd realize that America and Western industrialization has devastated earth life more than any other group. The magnitude of that depletion trivializes your suspect claim."

—JERRY, 32, white male

"The Chinese are not the reason the world population of tigers and whales is depleted. We are all to blame. I could make a list of countries that have helped in this, and the United States would be pretty high on it. Most of China is poor, so the people cannot afford the pills we in the West have to cure impotence. So they do what many poor people do worldwide: make their own. China is an old country with old habits. Things are changing in the large cities, but as you move out from them, you will see that life has not changed for years."

—EBONY, 23, black female

Y?Check

It's foolhardy to try to pin the endangerment of entire species of animals on "a bunch of old Chinese men trying to get an erection," says Michael Albertson, coauthor with his wife, Ellen, of *Food as Foreplay: Recipes for Romance, Love, and Lust* (Alexandria Press, 1998).

The Albertsons, hosts of the New England–area radio program *The Cooking Couple,* include extensive information about most aphrodisiacs on their website (www.cookingcouple.com), acknowledging that "many tiger parts (including the bones, liver, fat and penis) are considered to be very powerful aphrodisiacs in China."

However, Michael Albertson says he finds it more likely that "white European and American hunters and fishing conglomerates, and the expanding human population, have done a lot more damage to the animals and their habitats."

"I don't think old Chinese men had anything to do with the decimation of the American brown bear population in the nineteenth and early twentieth century," he points out. "My understanding of the tiger problem is that it has more to do with the almost total eradication of their natural habitats in China, India and Africa than erectile dysfunction.

"It seems to me the questioner is more interested in placing blame on a culture he does not understand as a way of not facing what his culture has done."

? ? ?

"**Why** do Americans appear unaware they are the most hated people on the planet?"

—ANDREINA, 31, female

Readers Respond

"We are the dominant country in the world. We help other countries with food, money and military support when we know we will never be reimbursed or even thanked. We do this because it's the right thing, not because it makes us the most popular."

—KATY, 38, white female

"I have traveled most of my life, and I have found that Americans overseas are made fun of, kidded, joked about and taken advantage of. In other words, they are treated just as foreigners anywhere are treated—no worse, and maybe a little bit better. Only a handful of ideologically backward countries—none of which would ever allow a forum like this one—consider America an evil, imperialist entity. Well, to hell with them."

—GREGG S., 43, American, Jewish

"The average American doesn't give a hoot about what goes on in the next state. They are self-centered, grazing cows with no ability to look beyond their frame of reference. I don't share the perspective of my compatriots, and it is very likely that one day I will leave this Land of Misguided Opportunity."

W.F., 29, dark male artist

"I am sure not all of us over here hate Americans. Of course, when they interfere in the internal affairs of our country without knowing the full historical details . . . But for the most part, we are grateful to the Americans for innovating everything from computer chips to satellites. Americans have been helpful to the world at large. Their actions, even though some may be self-centered, for the most part turn out to be good for the world. I will vote for Americans any day for the single reason that they are the guardians of democracy throughout the world."

—S. RAJAGOPAL, 21, Indian

"Americans are well aware we're hated—out of jealousy, misunderstanding or whatever. The fact is, we just don't care."

—RICK, male

"Haitians and Cubans ride leaky rafts to Miami for some reason. People dodge border guards to cross the Mexican-American border for some reason. The Chinese smuggle themselves onto cargo ships that dock in San Francisco for some reason. No, I'm not anti-immigrant. In fact, I have many immigrant friends. What I don't understand is the ambivalence among foreigners. We're the most hated, yet we're also the most requested."

—JOHN, male

Y? Check

Americans aren't hated by the rest of the world, according to Mark Hertsgaard, a veteran investigative journalist and author of *The Eagle's Shadow: Why America Fascinates and Infuriates the World* (Picador USA, 2003).

In fact, the average Yank is fairly well-liked overseas, he argues.

"The people of the United States are seen basically as friendly, optimistic and generous, if not terribly sophisticated and a little superficial . . . but they are very much admired," says Hertsgaard, who spent six months traveling the world before and after the September 11, 2001, terrorist attacks to research his book. "Our mass culture is emulated, and our ideals, the U.S. emblem of freedom and democracy, matter a lot overseas."

The U.S. government, however, is another story.

"We have become the richest and most powerful empire of the last half century, if not longer, and as a result we have unconsciously come to the conclusion that we can do what we want, when we want," Hertsgaard says. "But we learned from 9/11 that it's a little more complicated than that."

The U.S. media have played a major role in perpetuating the misconception that average Americans are despised, with its sloppy coverage in the aftermath of the terrorist attacks, scant attention paid to world events in general, failure to question the White House's march toward war with Iraq, and acceptance of the Bush administration's view that large chunks of the world hate Americans, he notes.

With most of the goodwill the United States gained after the attacks now evaporated, what's most disturbing to Hertsgaard is polling data showing that, for the first time, foreigners' enmity toward the U.S. government is starting to spill over into a more general negative view of America as a country.

Hertsgaard relates a story of an encounter with a businesswoman in Barcelona shortly after the 9/11 attacks that he says in many ways sums up the current worldview of America.

"She said: 'This is idiocy, we don't hate you! We have lived with your pop culture so long that it's our pop culture. I love Motown and Hollywood. I feel closer to Kansas than I do to Toulouse [a few hours away in France]. But we do wish our American friends would think a little more about your government, because we have to live with your government, and that's not always easy, especially now when war is in the air.' "

? ? ?

"The biggest culture shock I had when I went to the United States was when I walked into a public restroom. Why is the wide space necessary between the door and the floor? Aren't people ashamed of their legs being seen? And why do people put their stuff on the dirty floor? Also, aren't they ashamed of being heard when they are going to the bathroom? Some of them even talked to me while I was in there. I was so ashamed. In my country, there is a tape installed to block out the noise."

—KANAKO, 25, female

Readers Respond

"I'm with you! Although I've never lived anywhere else, I can't understand the lack of privacy in our public restrooms (and I'm a woman; I can't even imagine how the guys stand it). I went to Europe for the first time last year and thought it was great. All the stall doors went down to the floor, and they locked securely—no peeking under to check for feet. And I agree, while you're taking care of business is no time for a chat. It's just one of those things about my own culture that I just don't get."

—T.B., 20, white female

"If you grow up with it, of course you aren't going to be ashamed. At home, I share a community-style bathroom with many housemates—girls and guys—who hear me in the toilet stall and see me wrapped in a towel coming out of the shower. They do the same things in front of me. Maybe this has desensitized me, because the other day at work I used the toilet while a male janitor was in the restroom. I just really had to go."

—S.R., 21, white female

"While I think most people try to keep the noises to a minimum, to this American, it seems a little obsessive to play music to cover it up."

—STEVE, white male

"Unlike some Japanese women, most American women are not ashamed of their legs. They do not worry about daikon ashi ('radish legs' or fat calves)."

—R. DE LORIMIER, 31, white male

"I lived my whole life in Europe and only recently moved to the United States. What I found different here is that all toilets are already much more filled with water. Therefore, the sound effect is inevitable."

—MINA, white female

Y? Check

To understand this woman's confused reaction, one must understand just how different Japanese toilets and bathroom customs are from those in America, says Thomas Snitch, a consultant to Japanese business and government who holds a Ph.D. in international economics from The American University in Washington, D.C.

"First, Japanese toilets are in a separate room from the 'bathroom,' which contains a soaking tub. You would never find a toilet that was not in a closet or closed-off section in this area," says Snitch, who has worked with issues involving Japan and China for nearly three decades.

Second, Japanese toilets are basically squatting pans on the floor, unlike the raised bowls in America.

"Thus, to use them, you would lower yourself over the pan to the point that you would be very close to the floor," Snitch says. "You use the pan by facing it. If you were squatting and there was a large space between the floor and the bottom of the door, you would give everyone else a full view of . . ."

Third, to mask any embarrassing noises, women's toilets usually have a constantly running flow of water coursing through one of the toilets. Or if it is a Western-style toilet, as soon as you sit on the seat, a large amount of water begins to flow, creating a masking noise, he says. Indeed, many public bathrooms in urban areas are fitted with an "Otohime," made by Toto Ltd., which reproduces the sound of a flushing toilet to help drown out unpleasant restroom reverberations.

"In theory, because of the perceived loudness of the masking noise, it should be impossible to converse while in the stall, and no sounds should come out of your toilet area," Snitch continues. "Therefore, since no one talks in the toilet stall, everyone believes that no one could hear any noises coming out of their stall. Thus, we have harmony in the toilet area and no embarrassment."

Finally, the woman's comment about putting things on the floor relates to the Japanese custom of having everything in a proper place, he notes.

"When you enter a Japanese toilet, you remove the slippers you were wearing while in the rooms of the house and put on 'toilet slippers.' These are *only* used in the toilet and, when you exit, the slippers remain at the door of the toilet and you put your regular slippers back on. Therefore, there is no danger of tracking anything unsightly back into the living area from the toilet pan area."

No one would take anything into a public stall in Japan, anyway, he said; they would leave their shopping bags on a shelf outside.

"You certainly would not soil a package that you might give as a gift by bringing it into a toilet stall," Snitch says. "Japan is a safe country—you don't have to worry about your packages being stolen while you are in the toilet, since this is simply never done."

? ? ?

"**Why** do people think that people in the Midwest are all boring, uncultured idiots?"

—B., 28, male

Readers Respond

"Because they are. Having been born in Kansas and grown up in Iowa and Illinois, and having just come home from an obligatory visit, I am realizing anew how much I hate the Midwest. It is a region of incurious and intolerant—though seemingly friendly, at least if you're white and American—idiots. They hate and fear anything unusual. They are racists and bigots. They are too lazy to really think about things or form their own opinions through experience. They get their news and views from *USA Today,* their food from fast-food franchises and their household goods from Wal-Mart."

—OUTTATHERE

"To Outtahere: Sounds nothing like anywhere I have been (Nebraska, Iowa, Missouri, Minnesota, Illinois, Kansas, Colorado and the list goes on). It sounds to me like you moved West, started making a little more money and forgot what The Good Life is all about."

—SUMMER, 20, white female

"Here are some things I've had a lot of trouble finding every time I've ventured into our nation's middle: excellent ethnic restaurants. Unusual book stores. Theaters specializing in foreign and/or independent films. Neighborhoods full of art galleries. Decent coffee. Good radio."

—ANDREW, 35, white male

"In Minneapolis there are large Somali and Hmong communities that are, for the most part, accepted and included. We are also home to a great university with a proud medical and intellectual tradition.

Northern Minnesota is home to a number of nature-loving people (I include hunters in this group). If failing to shop at the local vegan mart or bomb fast-food franchises in some spirited protest of globalization is your version of cultural stagnation, then greater Minnesota might not be the place for you, but most Minnesotans I know are commonsensical, tolerant and generally just good people."

—BERNIE, 17, white female

"I have never found such a boring, generic place as the Midwest. Having been in Minneapolis for three years, I think I have given the Midwest a good opportunity to prove me otherwise. Unless you went to the University of St. Thomas (for some fucking reason they think it is in the same league as Harvard—hate to tell you 'Tommies,' but go 1,000 miles in either direction and no one has ever heard of you) and have a ton of family, this is one of the most unfriendly places I have ever been. 'Minnesota nice'—yeah, whatever. Try the land of the practical haircuts and fat asses."

—STELLABLUE, 36, female

Y ? C heck

You could blame Hollywood or TV network moguls in New York, but the Midwest's image problem started before either was around.

"It isn't an accident," says Edward Watts, who teaches American Thought at Michigan State University and studies the Midwest's heritage.

Watts says the region was expected from its infancy to play second fiddle to East Coast cities like Boston and New York and has been living with an inferiority complex for more than a century.

From Sherwood Anderson's stories about small-town Ohio life to the Iowa baseball field for ghost players in the movie *Field of Dreams,* the region's image has been like a shrine to America's homespun past, expected to stay frozen in time.

"This is a place that's not supposed to change," says Watts, who wrote about the region's identity in *An American Colony: Regionalism and Roots of Midwestern Culture* (Ohio University Press, 2002). "This is the most American of all places, according to that legend."

The reality is a lot more complex. Academics at Ohio State University have been preparing the *Encyclopedia of the Midwest,* in print and online form, with hopes of describing a more complete identity. Sections dealing with culture will try to show there are many different kinds of cultural resources, from Chicago's museums to Cleveland's Rock and Roll Hall of Fame to Native American mound sites.

? ? ?

"Can someone please tell me why the French have such reputations for being rude?"

—TERRI, 33, white female

Readers Respond

"I went to France one recent summer. I did find the French sometimes do have a superiority complex, thinking that theirs, whatever it is, is the best. But I let that go because I found that indeed many things they felt strongly about were better—their food, fashion, perfume . . ."

—SARAH

"Most people get their view of French people from visiting Paris—the most-visited city in the world, with tens of millions of visitors per year. Most Parisians have had more than their daily fill of rude tourists who act like they own the town, and act as though the locals have nothing better to do than stop and give directions 15 times on their way to lunch."

—LORIN, 31, white male

"French people are more direct than Americans, dispensing with sugar-coating any information."

—KARLA O., 42, American of French descent

"My staff and I do employment and educational verifications worldwide. Most people we call (if we don't speak the language) will go out of their way to help us. I have called several French universities (where to attend you must have taken English classes), and they will speak French only and hang up if I speak English. If you don't believe me, call the Registrar's Office at Université Claude Bernard in Lyon and try speaking English only."

—K. FREMIN

"The French are very different from Americans, but it's a complementary difference. We excel at commercial values, while the French have greater respect for intellect and esthetic than any people I've met. Yes, they are rude, but they are among themselves even more so than with Americans. If you can return insults, it becomes something of a sport. One such encounter: In Le Havre one Sunday, the restaurants were closed, and I was traveling with two English guys. We went into a bar, and while I was asking the bartender about sandwiches, one of the English guys opened the ice cream freezer to see what kinds of packaged snacks were inside. The bartender yelled for him to stop, then added, *'Nous nous foutons de vous les etrangers!'* ('We don't give a fuck about you foreigners!') Purely by inspiration, I shouted back, *'Sans nos peres, vous parleriez l'allemand!'* ('Without our fathers, you'd be speaking German!') We left feeling quite pleased with the incident, and my French friends have always liked the story, because the bartender was a type they recognized and of course opposed, personally and politically."

—JERRY C., male

Y?Check

What's brusque in one culture might not be in another, according to Laura K. Lawless, a French language guide and moderator of the French site at About.com.

"There are polite people and there are rude people in every country, city and street on Earth," says Lawless, a French translator who has lived in France and visits there regularly.

The key to a pleasant visit is the French language, she says. Learn at least some before you go and you'll do yourself and the natives a favor.

"If nothing else, know how to say *bonjour* (hello) and *merci* (thank you), and as many polite terms like please and excuse me as possible. Don't tap someone on the shoulder and say, 'Hey, where's the Louvre?' " she says. "English . . . is far from the only language, and the French in particular expect visitors to know this."

As well, don't perpetuate the myth of the "ugly American" by being one, Lawless says. Yelling at everyone in English, griping about anything French, and insisting on le Quarter Pounder avec fromage (with cheese) isn't going to help matters.

"Showing respect for another culture means enjoying what it has to offer, rather than searching for signs of one's own home," Lawless says. "If you are respectful of the French and their heritage, they will respond in kind."

Still, some feel the French are rude without a word even being uttered, and Lawless says that's based on a misunderstanding of the French persona. Americans are one of a number of cultures that automatically smile when they meet new people. The French don't smile unless they mean it, she says.

"And they don't smile when talking to a perfect stranger. Therefore, when an American smiles at a French person whose face remains impassive, the former tends to feel that the latter is unfriendly," Lawless says. "[But] it's simply the way of the French."

? ? ?

"While growing up in the South I've often noticed that when two males attend a movie together, they often leave a seat open between them. Is this a regional practice or is it seen throughout the United States?"

MERRIMAN, female

Readers Respond

"When I was growing up in New York, guys who went to the movies together always kept an empty seat between them if they could.

They'd put their popcorn and drinks on it, but that's not the reason for the seat. Guys laughingly called it 'the fag seat' or the 'I'm not a fag' seat. Insecure blue-collar New Yorkers that we were, we thought it was somehow unmasculine to sit next to a male friend."

—ASTORIAN, straight male

"I think it has to do with the fear of someone thinking the guys are gay. My friends and I never leave a seat between us in a movie. I was raised in the North and currently live in the South. No seat splitting here."

—BRIAN, male

"I've grown up in the Chicago area and now live in California, and I've seen the same in both areas. As an adult male, I usually leave a seat between any person unless it's very crowded or I'm sitting next to my wife. Two of the reasons are I would be bumping shoulders, arms and legs if they were in the next seat, and there would be competition for the armrest. Of course, if it is an attractive woman, those would be the very same reasons I would sit next to her."

—ROB, 35, white male

"Personal space! If there is the option to spread out and be totally relaxed while you enjoy the movie, then people are going to take it. It's not because we're afraid of being seen as gay. It's just that if I want to stretch my arms in the middle of the movie, I don't think my friend would like it if I punched him in the face in the process."

—PAUL, 19

Y? Check

It's far-fetched to think Southern men are more likely than other men to sit apart in a darkened movie theater, says Kevin Johnston, whose doctoral work at the University of Tennessee–Knoxville focused on the changing concepts of Southern masculinity.

However, that's not to say that *any* male in the South might not be more aware of which behaviors mesh best with his particular community's shared notion of Southern manhood.

That, in turn, could influence a man's decision on whether to rub elbows at the flicks—or use a "missing man" seating formation.

Such "unwritten but understood" rules of masculinity can play a crucial role in the behavior of men (Southern or not), often to seemingly paradoxical ends.

"Two or three men conscious of how they might appear sitting together in a theater could be the same three who instinctively slap each other's derriéres in the showers after a good game," Johnston says.

Complicating things even more is the fact that standards of manhood in the South have blurred with those of the country's as a whole.

Johnston adds that while there is still unquestionably a concept of "Southern manhood," it is in most cases less historically distinct today than it was in the nineteenth and most of the twentieth century, yet "not surprisingly, they carry as many stereotypical notions about what it means to be from the South as do outsiders observing Southern social interaction."

? ? ?

"**Why** is sex with children legal in Japan? How do the Japanese feel about Rorikon—Japanese for 'Lolita complex'?"

—J.

Readers Respond

"The main reason is that until recently, it wasn't common enough to merit attention. If it did occur, typically the couple would be either seeking a marriage or forced into it. Since the economic depression of the '80s, times have changed. An increasing phenomenon is the practice of 'compensated dating,' in which an older man pays a younger girl to be his girlfriend. The awareness of this is growing in Japan, and unprecedented laws are being passed to prohibit it. Ironically, it's the girls who end up having to pay the penalty, which is usually a hefty fine."

—EDWARD, 31, male

"It's not legal, although as far as I know the minimum age for girls is set at the local level and varies from place to place. I seem to remember it being upped from 14 in the place where I lived after the outcry over schoolgirl prostitution. I think the whole attraction to young girls comes from Anime and Manga comic books (or did *that* come from an attraction to young girls?). The Japanese like cute stuff, and all girls think school uniforms, short skirts, pigtails, etc. are cute, so it kind of fuels itself."

—STEPHEN, male

"I lived in Japan for two years and recently traveled to Japan and saw many junior and high school girls taking part in 'Compo-Dato' (compensated dating). Thus, a 12- or 13-year-old girl arranges a date with a sariman (salaryman) through the dating service available through her cell phone company. She makes about $2,000 for her first time, and about $500 each time thereafter. Rorikon has been alive and well in Japanese culture for a long time. Many TV movies and magazine features aimed at teen girls and guys, as well as adults, featured rape of a young female teen as an approved highlight of the movie or article. This was later exploited to have the male fantasy realized, in the mid- to late-'90s. (Japanese men and some Americans have been going on child or teen sex tours in Thailand for a long time. I saw it firsthand in Bangkok.) Ultimately, I believe the exploding sex industry in Japan has to do with youth rebellion and a sexist culture with values both different and similar to Western values. At the prison where I work in the United States, about 50 percent are locked up for sex crimes that are openly accepted in Japan. There is no simple analysis of Japan's sex scene; I'm only offering my observances from living there. I hope this wonderful country will find her own answers that stop abuse of young females."

—ANNETTE, 41, white female

Y? Check

The age of consent in Japan is thirteen, but for several years the country has been adding laws to combat child prostitution and sexual abuse of the young. Under international pressure to reform, Japan's parliament banned child pornography in 1999 and criminalized some sex. Another law was added in 2003 to forbid soliciting sex from minors over the Internet.

This has been a delicate subject for some Japanese, according to the Associated Press and other worldwide media reports, particularly after the Internet's emergence in the 1990s exposed the country's porn industry to a global market. Before the laws began changing, there were estimates that up to 80 percent of the web's child porn came from Japan. More recently, police had reported a spike in crimes tied to personal ads on the Internet, with teenage girls often becoming victims. A number of young girls became prostitutes, sometimes telling police later that they wanted spending money or were simply curious.

Under the 1999 legislation, a person who pays for sex with a child or distributes child porn could serve up to three years in prison, and a pimp could serve five years. Anyone who buys a child for sex could serve ten years.

Passage of the 1999 legislation was politically difficult and required years of lobbying by female lawmakers. Since then, there have been reports of government officials, even police, being caught in situations that involved young girls.

Still in Question

A Sampling of Culture- and Geographic-Related Questions
Seeking Answers at Y? (www.yforum.com)

"Why are less-intelligent characters always portrayed as Southerners by television, movie and screen writers? Deliverance wasn't a documentary."

—CURTIS J., 40, white male

"It's my impression that Canadians in general are very poor tippers. Why is this?"

—C.S.M., 27

"I'm in a relationship with a Vietnamese man who believes he loses his 'essence' when having an orgasm. He also believes too much sex makes a man age. Is this true of the whole Vietnamese culture?"

—LAURIE S., 48, bisexual white female

"Within the last year I came in contact with two Russian females. They both are feisty, nosy, hot-tempered and sometimes just flat-out rude. Is this coincidence, or do Russian females have attitudes, sort of like black females?"

—JAY, 21, white male

"Why is it that Southern women appear so superficial, over-groomed and manipulative?"

—SANDRA, 35, female

"To Chinese people, or people who work in a Chinese restaurant: Do you kill cats, cook them and sell them to your customers, stating that it is chicken? Please be honest."

—ELIZABETH S., 23, mixed race female

"Are Germans more militaristic and more obsessed with neatness and cleanliness than other people?"

—LENORA, 44, white female

"Northerners seem to be almost afraid of black people, but Southerners don't. Why is this?"

—MELISSA, 22, white female

"What does it mean when an American calls someone a 'French whore'?"

—JULIE, 22, white female

SEVEN

Looking Up,
Looking Down:

Class

"**Friends** and acquaintances (basically white-collar, middle-class) say they would prefer not to date blue-collar, working-class people because the differences in values and goals are too difficult to overcome. How common is this attitude?"

—D., female

"Call me elitist, but I would not date or marry someone outside my class. I divorced someone blue-collar; I'm white-collar, upper-middle class and have a master's degree–plus. I really disliked his poor-mouthing, his feeling of being exploited by the haves while he was a have-not. I met my current husband online, during an e-mail discussion on literature. He's more open to options in life, as well as a better creative thinker."

—KATIE, 31, teacher

"As a temp worker, I am consistently amazed at how little 'educated' upper-class, white-collar people know about anything other than how to keep their picket fences white and their lawns perfectly green.

These are people who make more a year than I do in five, yet wouldn't know the difference between Bukowski and Berkowitz and believe Turkey is nothing more than something you have on Thanksgiving. As far as money is concerned, there is so much more to life than overpriced theater tickets, expensive restaurants and trips to the South of France."

—BRIAN, 33

"More blue-collar people live their lives with fewer dreams than their white-collar counterparts. Privilege brings a sense that you can accomplish anything, and working at jobs where you use your hands instead of your mind does limit the scope of your dreams."

—S. FINCH, 37, white female

"My first husband was from a more financially successful family than mine. He wanted to go to law school and even had a vacation home in the mountains. His father was a judge. He also had an overwhelming credit card debt, a habit of letting his parents pick up the tab and an inability to recognize the good in me or himself. After three years, he said he was not ready for this kind of commitment and walked out. After the divorce, I dated various men—oddly, most had no college education—and finally married (happily now for three years) a man with no advanced education who is smart and witty and who reads everything he can find. He manages a warehouse. He is kind, generous, loving, honest and terribly funny—he is also not in debt or attached to his mother's apron strings."

—SHEILA, 27, white

Y?Check

Collar color and socioeconomic background don't matter in a long-term relationship if both partners have discussed the matter and mapped out their priorities beforehand, says Randi Minetor, researcher and author of *Breadwinner Wives and the Men They Marry: How to Have a Successful Marriage While Outearning Your Husband* (New Horizon Press, 2002).

Minetor surveyed couples who were in relationships similar to hers: She's a white-collar professional and earns more than her husband, who works in lighting design. She found that more than class or job status, the level of one's education is the prevailing factor in how well these types of relationships work.

"Chances are a Ph.D. is not going to marry someone who has no college," she says. "There's a similarity of intellect and experience from being in college that separates people who haven't had that experience . . . there's a period of immersing oneself in study and preparing for a career, and if you haven't done that and just started working out of high school, that person has a different point of view . . . it's tougher to find common ground."

Even when education levels differ, problems often can be resolved inside the marriage, Minetor says. It's the pressure that mounts from outside sources that can sometimes become too much to bear.

"An example is one couple I interviewed: She has a degree and is a computer analyst, and he's a farmer. They found it was not really an issue—she makes money, he builds his business. But her parents are mortified she would marry so far beneath herself. One sister even said, 'Look at his life, is that the life you want for yourself?' And she was like, 'Yeah, I love him.' "

Couples that reconcile an imbalance in career, money, or education—and many do find happiness, Minetor says—have made the effort to seek out what each partner brings of greatest value to the table.

"The values and goals for the relationship and family are really what's important. The most successful of these couples emphasize the good things that are brought to the relationship. A blue-collar guy who works with his hands, an electrician or a plumber, well, they can build the addition on the house . . . there are many other qualities besides what you make or what you grew up with."

? ? ?

"**To** people who have been both poor and rich, I read a study that surprised me: The richest people rated themselves as only slightly happier than the poorest people. Does that finding hold true for you?"

—GERRY, 34, white male, middle class, Fort Worth, TX

Readers Respond

"There is something comforting about coming home to a neighborhood with paved streets and sidewalks where folks aren't hanging out on the corner. There is something that makes me happy to open the refrigerator and see food in plenty of supply. There is something that makes me happy to realize that when my shoes have holes, I can pay to have the shoemaker repair them and not just stick something water-resistant inside. There is something comforting about being able to run an air-conditioner in the summer or not worry that if I leave my windows open that someone will come in and harm me. Money has made all the difference in my world. Money buys safety, and that is a basic human need."

—ANNE, 39, Jewish female, middle class

"If you can't taste the miracle of hot tomato soup after a February day working as a mover's helper in the rain, you probably can't taste the miracle of a perfect rack of lamb in a four-star Paris restaurant."

—JOHN B., white male, upper middle class, rural area

"I have been a 22-year-old making more than $50,000 a year, as well as a broke, in-debt, 24-year-old unable to afford a car or rent, eating 50-cent black beans from a can. Here's the kicker: Money is interesting in that with it, you can afford to pretend that life does not suck."

—MR. DICKERSON, 25, white male, middle class

"Grandpa died a few years back and left me $30,000. Not a fortune, but a nice chunk; didn't worry about groceries, paying rent, bought the piano I wanted, paid for college, forgot to cash my regular paycheck twice, but never got laid during this time. Been poor: Living off credit cards and minimum wage, wondering how to pay for food, debt stacked up, lack of options, staying home every night 'cause of no money, and never got laid. Bottom line: Rich is better . . . and I don't get laid much."

—CHRIS B., 34, white male, middle class

"I was raised in a *very* wealthy family. You lose sight of what it is to be a normal person when you are raised with more money than you know what to do with. You don't need to keep up with the Joneses. That is a real fallacy of the so-called American dream. Decide what is real and what is not. And most of all, what is really important."

—LINDSAY, 49, white female, self-employed

Y? Check

Research shows that rich people are generally just a bit happier than average folks, who in turn are a bit happier than poor people, says Ed Diener, a psychologist at the University of Illinois at Urbana–Champaign who has spent decades measuring people's happiness.

"We studied people from the *Forbes* list of richest Americans and found that their life satisfaction was fairly high, but not anywhere close to the top of the scale," he says.

Money matters when it delivers decent food and housing, security, and opportunities to have a more rounded life. But the fact that the country overall is vastly wealthier than fifty years ago, yet not giddily cheerful about it, is often given as big-picture proof that satisfaction is about more than dollars and cents. Many researchers talk about people's "subjective well-being," a measurement that acknowledges complex personal yardsticks for happiness.

That doesn't mean everyone's fantasy about life as a Lotto winner is all wrong. It's just incomplete.

"We are currently studying people whose income goes up dramatically, and they do get happier," Diener explains. "But they end up not any happier than people whose income goes up slowly over time. People's happiness may jump up substantially if they win the lottery or receive another type of windfall, but over time they get used to their level of income and the 'high' wears off.

"Other factors such as temperament and good, quality social relationships seem to be much more important than money. One other interesting finding is that materialistic people, those who place a higher value on money than other things such as love, seem to suffer in terms of lower well-being, although a very high income can offset this effect to some degree."

? ? ?

"Recently I met a man in college who claims to be a skinhead. His head is shaven, and he wears camouflage and a flak jacket and steel-toed boots. However, he claims not to be racist. He says skinheads are just 'working-class culture,' whatever that means. Does anyone know what he is talking about, or should I retire to my original idea of jumping him?"

—SEAMUS, 21, male

Readers Respond

"What characterizes a skinhead has less to do with their feelings on race and more with their feelings on society as a whole. A skinhead has a certain look. Most have a bald head, and many wear 'pork chop' sideburns. They often dress in tight jeans, certain types of shirts and combat boots. Unless your friend is proudly displaying a swastika or listening to bands like Skrewdriver, you have no reason to think he's a racist. In fact, I know some black skinheads who'd be pretty upset if they were lumped into that category."

—ANONYMOUS, 25, white female

"I'm a skinhead, and my parents were skinheads. It has bugger all to do with racism! That's just neo-Nazi bonehead scum. The media always identifies race hate with skinheads, but it's not true—the boneheads stole our culture (but not our style) in the mid-late '70s. Real skins have a style and culture mixed from the United Kingdom and Jamaica. Check out the ska music circa '69: Symarip's 'Skinhead

Moonstomp' or The Pioneers' 'Reggae Fever' and God knows how many other reggae skinhead classics—before any bonehead white noise."

—JASON, 31, mixed race skinhead

"Even non-racist skins can be rather ignorant; S.H.A.R.P.s (Skinheads Against Racial Prejudice) can be a little too patriotic, denouncing immigrants no matter their color, and can be a little fascist in their political views (anti-Communist or anti-anarchist), though I have met many S.H.A.R.P.s who were very non-racist and genuinely kind people."

—RATCHET

Y? Check

Skinheads are united in their bald pates, workboots, rowdiness, and even violence, but not all are racist, says Mark Potok, editor of the Montgomery, Alabama–based Southern Poverty Law Center's renowned *Intelligence Report,* which documents right-wing hate groups.

In fact, a good chunk of their membership in the United States today is passionately against racism, he says.

"There are a significant number of anti-racist (skinheads) who like nothing better than to mix it up with the Nazis," Potok notes.

The entire movement began in the late 1960s in Liverpool and London. Youths wore steel-toed Doc Martens boots, donned Fred Perry British street clothes, shaved their heads in homage to their working-class roots, and adopted aspects of Jamaican culture such as ska and reggae music from new immigrants to the area.

"The whole shaved heads thing related to the idea of their dads, who were working in factories where they needed to shave their heads so they didn't get pulled into machinery," Potok says. "The steel-toed boots were so that if some ingot drops on your toes, you won't be lame the rest of your life."

From the beginning, a common thread was violence.

"There was a lot of beer drinking, bars, women and drugs. It was very much in opposition to what they saw as the middle-class rich kids."

In the 1970s, however, neo-fascist groups led by the National Front co-opted a portion of the skinheads movement, hoping to use their members as shock troops in a "revolution and race war," Potok says.

A rift in the skinheads developed, and when the movement migrated to the United States in the early 1980s, that split came with it intact—S.H.A.R.P.s representing one end of the spectrum and hardcore racists such as Hammerskins representing the other.

The number of skinheads in the United States is down since their heyday, but there are still around 10,000 nationwide—with a sizable minority that are nonracist, Potok adds.

Nowadays, he says, it's not at all unusual for a local racist skinhead concert to end up in a pitch street battle between racist and nonracist factions—or with "a hell of a lot of cops trying to keep the two apart."

? ? ?

"I was in a grocery store and noticed several people in the checkout lanes with thick gold jewelry and expensive Nike apparel. But they were paying with food stamps. Even their small children were wearing expensive clothes. Why is this?"

—JESSICA G., female

Readers Respond

"I received food stamps for a short time. Just hang out at any food stamp issuing office and listen to the conversations—many people are hiding income to receive benefits, or selling the stamps they receive. Besides the obvious greed, many of these people need immediate gratification, and that is why many of them will be 'poor' for the rest of their lives."

—KARIN, 32

"I lived in Los Angeles all my life, and there was never a shortage of food stamp customers before me in line. I have to eat frozen burritos and canned veggies, but they seem to be able to afford the most expensive cuts of meat and lobster. I once followed a lady out to her car and asked if I could have something from her bag that I paid for."

—CYD E., 34, white working male

"I am a single mother of one small child. I receive food stamps. We buy our clothes and toys and many other things at Goodwill and the Salvation Army. Mine don't look so good, but my son's look very nice because the donated kids' clothing was outgrown before it was worn out. Before I got laid off, before I became a parent, before a lot of things, I sometimes felt resentful of people with food stamps who looked like they 'had something.' Now I can tell it from the other side: To qualify for food stamps is painful. To use them hurts. To be recertified for them is humiliating."

—HUMBLED, 39, white female

"When I was raising my two daughters by myself, I worked two to three part-time jobs in addition to attending college full-time. There is no safe ground for the working poor. If those same people in the grocery store had been dressed poorly, you would have judged them for that ('Look how poorly they are groomed. Why don't they take better care of themselves and their children?'). I know. I have heard it all."

—RACHAEL, 44, white female

"For every Henri Bendel department store there is a Nordstrom Rack or Filene's Basement, where over-priced fashionable gear can be purchased at a fraction of the cost."

—SHE THING, black female

"I received food stamps. I was a single mother with Lupus. Though I come from a two-parent, hard-working family, I could not work, and had to accept help from the government. I never felt bad about it because I knew this was the reason I had paid taxes as a teenager working for very little money. Just because I qualified for food stamps, I saw no need to let my child look uncared-for. Nike is not expensive. Prada is expensive. 12-karat gold jewelry is not expensive. Platinum is expensive."

—C. PHILLIPS, 25, black female

Y?Check

A never-ending debate for federal and state governments is how to help the needy and still spot frauds trying to chisel a piece of the action.

Well-dressed people using food stamps might or might not be cheating, but there's always some waste, fraud, and abuse in the system. In 2003, more than 22 million Americans were enrolled for food stamps, which use a sliding income scale to help people living near or below the poverty line afford decent, cheap meals.

The U.S. Department of Agriculture estimated about 2.5 cents of every dollar of food stamps issued between 1999 and 2002 was sold below face value for cash instead of food. That's about $395 million in illegal trafficking per year. Neighborhood grocery store owners have been caught trafficking stamps, and investigators use computer programs to look for suspicious redemption patterns. It's much harder to spot occasional trades between individuals, although police sometimes bust street-corner drug dealers who accept food stamps like cash.

Overall, most poor people would just end up poorer selling their stamps at a discount, so it's not their first preference, says James Ohls, an economist at Mathematica Policy Research, Inc., a New Jersey research center that often studies food stamp issues.

"If you were about to get evicted, you might do that because you need money immediately," he says, or a trusted friend might make a deal to use some stamps during hard times.

? ? ?

"**Why** does it seem that many members of the Jewish community have a lot of money, power and smarts?"

—G. CHAN, 18, Asian male

Readers Respond

"Until recently, Jews were discriminated against when looking for work, so they had to become self-employed by opening a business or becoming a doctor, etc. And you know the saying, 'You never get rich working for someone else.' "

—RONIT, 38, Jewish female

"It's true that Jews have a disproportionate representation in the media and in many high-profile occupations. It's not a plot to take over the world. It's just a culturally ingrained drive to excel. There is a stereotype that Jews only help each other, though, and that is not true. Many Jews put themselves on the frontlines during the Civil Rights movement in the '60s and have been active in countless other causes."

—THEO, 30, white female

"Jews are God's chosen people. They have the God-given ability to succeed, and whatever they do turns to gold. They are also hard workers and very shrewd."

—EVE, black female, Pentecostal

"Because of anti-Semitism, Jews around the world were banned from certain occupations, land ownership, etc. Therefore, Jews were forced into service occupations, such as medicine, law and teaching, all of which require extensive education."

—RACHEL Z., 52, Jewish female

"Jews from a very early age are taught to question authority and think sharply. Judaism encourages questions and investigation, which is why Jews are always thinking of what to do next. In addition, Jews are brought up with good moral standards. It is easier to focus on success when you are not consumed with drugs, alcohol and sex. As kids we are discouraged from watching TV, but rather focus on schoolwork and community service. The main reason Jews are so smart is because we follow God, and only good things can come from that."

—ITA, 22, white female, Jewish

Y?Check

On average, members of the Jewish community rank high economically in America, Canada, Great Britain, and other places that offer high levels of opportunity, says Kenneth Wald, director of Jewish Studies at the University of Florida. In the United States, they rank second only to Hindu Americans, many of whom arrive with higher education or advanced degrees, he says.

Although the notion of money and power among Jews is exaggerated, the seed of truth to this broad stereotype comes from the immigrant heritage of many European and Israeli Jews, he notes: Parents of first-generation Americans pushed education as "the passport" to a better life, something Wald's parents did in his early years in Nebraska.

"My parents made a conscious decision not to speak German at home. They didn't want us to be hindered in any way in our education, and it was pounded into our heads when I was a kid that we had to get a great education," he says. "We never had the question of whether we would go on to college."

Devout immersion in their religion might also help, Wald says.

"The study of the Torah has always been seen as something taught to the children . . . so everyone had to read," he says. "During the Bar Mitzvah or Bas Mitzvah, the young person stands before the congregation and not only reads from the text, but is expected to give a sermon on that portion. We are talking about 12- and 13-year-old boys and girls."

But Wald says he doesn't think Jewish people have more power than other ethnic groups that value economic status and higher education.

"Jews are a very political people . . . they tend to be over-involved in registering to vote and running for office, and that in part is because they have strong beliefs that can be advanced in a political system like ours," he says. "But what worries more Jews is that there is a main argument used by non-Jews of this Jewish power structure that runs the country. Jews are very sensitive about not being known as the finger that controls the world."

Prejudice can serve as a strong motivator, though, he adds.

"My parents very strongly told me I would have to be twice as good to get as far as a non-Jew, and [that I should] take for granted that there were people who would want to keep me out because I was Jewish," Wald says. "This perception is another reason why immigrant groups work harder to get ahead, because they don't feel people will give it to them on a silver platter. But this seems to have diminished. Neither of my children feels there is any disadvantage whatsoever."

Still in Question
A Sampling of Class-Related Questions
Seeking Answers at Y? (www.yforum.com)

"Do people who live in expensive houses on hills that overlook a city feel superior to those who live below?"

—TOM

"What types of class and power structures do homeless communities institute and follow among themselves? This culture must fend for itself, so I imagine its members follow some unwritten codes for survival. What are they?"

—ED V., 37

"I am an emergency services worker, so I get to all parts of town. Can anyone tell me why, the poorer the neighborhood, the more trash and broken bottles litter the streets?"

—JON E., male

"Why do some people want to live in a gated community, even in places where crime isn't out of hand?"

—M.S.H., average income

"If the meek inherit the earth, and pride goeth before a fall, where is the dividing line? Where is the division between humility and being a martyr; or being self-confident vs. vain? What are indications of each? Is dressing well and pride in appearance vain, or should we all be wearing gunny sacks for the sake of humility? Is it humble to have only what one needs and vain to have what one wants?"

—KATHY E., 45

"Why is it that in ghettos and 'hoods with a majority of black residents, you always see sneakers hanging off the telephone wires?"

—TYLER, 14, white male

"Do people from poorer neighborhoods feel uncomfortable when visiting more affluent neighborhoods?"

—CANDICE, 18, Asian female

EIGHT

Out with It:

Sex and Sexual Orientation

"To gay people: How and when did you know you were gay?"

—SUE A., 38

Readers Respond

"For me, I knew when in 1968 I was taken to see the movie *Doctor Zhivago*. When Omar Sharif came on the screen, I thought I'd been hit by a ton of bricks. Even though I didn't know exactly what I was feeling, I knew something was going on. I figured it out about 14 years later."

—DAVID R., 38

"I was first aware of being different from my twin sister when we were in about the first grade. By third grade I was certain I was very different, attracted very strongly to girls and not to boys at all. It caused a lot of difficulty because I had a tendency to 'steal' my sister's best friends."

—DARLENE C.

"I knew as early as age 5 that I was gay. I was raised in a fundamental Christian home and never missed a service. I taught Sunday school, was the music director and the youth leader in our church. So it was not due to a lack of religious training."

—STEVE N., 40, gay male

"I finally fell in love with a very persistent suitor in college who ironically enough liked me because I was different, not boy crazy like other girls. We married and moved to Nebraska. I responded sexually to my husband's lovemaking. I dismissed any romantic interest in women as simple sexual curiosity that would go away if ignored. But of course it didn't, even though I remained devoutly monogamous. His extra-marital affair the third year of our marriage broke my heart. As a political and social activist, I met many lesbian feminists. By the time my husband had another serious affair, we had grown so far apart that he came to cry on my shoulder when his married lover wanted to break up with him. After 18 years of marriage, I wanted my freedom. Coming out as a lesbian has been one of the most wonderfully freeing, emotionally fulfilling experiences of my life."

—DYKEONBYKE, 48, late-blooming lesbian

"I enjoyed being in the cloak room with 'Steven.' I enjoyed the night in Scout Camp when Rick asked if I wanted to touch his erection. I had a deep crush on John in high school. I cared deeply about Walt in college. None of this made sense to me until I finally met a man (Mike) and realized that I love men."

—STEVE W.

Y? Check

"There's no point in time when we can stamp you on the forehead and say 'if you were going to be gay, you'd know by now,' " says Lisa M. Diamond, a University of Utah psychologist who studies gay/lesbian sexuality and how affection develops between people.

Diamond says some people begin having gay feelings in junior high school, while others might have them after they're middle-aged, married, and raising children. It was once assumed that people who came out late had been repressed, but she says the real lesson may be that people aren't necessarily hard-wired for one orientation through-out their lives.

Diamond thinks that's especially true of women, whose sex lives are, on average, more tied to individual romantic relationships than men's are.

"There's a lot of evidence that women's sexuality is just more fluid than men's," she says, adding that women describing how they became lesbians are more likely to mention a pivotal relationship with one woman, while gay men will often report an attraction to men in general.

For people who think they're gay, changing times have made it easier to find out about some of the emotional and identity issues in-volved. While gays who came out a generation ago often have stories about nervously seeking information at a bookstore or library, coun-terparts today can find volumes of information on the Internet with less anxiety about scrutiny from outsiders. That's especially impor-tant for people in rural areas or adolescents with no car to reach the bookstore, Diamond says.

Even with better information, recognizing you're gay can carry a lot of baggage, especially for adolescents who often hide their feelings from parents and school friends. Diamond says there's a huge age range for people's first gay experiences. Some realize they are gay from the time they're teenagers, but others not until middle age or later. Although some people might expect that changing times mean fewer late-bloomers, Diamond says there's good reason to think some people's sexuality just changes partway through their lives.

Changing times also haven't necessarily made it easier for young people to come to terms with being gay. Diamond says spending time with other gay teens can help them see themselves in a better light, but a lot of kids don't have access to that social network. Some high schools have gay/straight clubs that provide a social outlet, but the same kinds of clubs have been vigorously discouraged in other places, she says.

? ? ?

"**I** had a girlfriend one time in the shower take my hand and place it on her crotch. She then urinated on my hand and asked me to play with her at that time. Why would anyone do this? This ended our two-year relationship because I was not understanding. This question has been hounding me for years."

—NICK, early 30s, white male

Readers Respond

"My temptation is to say that any woman who is into this is seriously disturbed. However, that is probably just my own uptightness. It is a fetish, with no more logic or appeal to an outsider than any other fetish."

—D.M.M., white female

"You don't need that girl. I think she was crazy for thinking you would like that. I would never pee on you or anyone else!"

—JLGM56, female

"I can't believe I read this question. Hello Nick. This is Dana (a joke name between Nick and I). I fell over in my chair when I read your question. I hope you are the Nick I dated for two years in _____! I knew this bugged you after I did what I did. But to me, I really do enjoy it. It is a rush. The areas around the female urethra are very close to the clitoris on some women. To have a urine stream stopped by someone else or by yourself is very much a turn-on. It even tickles. It may not do the same to males, but I know it is a turn-on to many women. I had to research this just to ensure I was not a pervert, and I did find out many people do practice this type of sexual foreplay. To me, it is foreplay for better sex afterward. It just feels great. What else can I say? I still work at the same place if you want to stop by."

—NOPE, female

"As a very sexually active woman, I see no way that being played with while peeing would bring any pleasure."

—NIKKI, female

"I enjoy this. It turns my husband on. We discovered it by accident when I wet him during sex. It has been part of our sex as much as possible since. It is less messy than having sex during your period, and I know more women do that than are willing to admit."

—GAIL, late 30s, female

Y? Check

There are two main camps of people who like to pee on other people, says Dr. Gloria G. Brame, an Athens, Georgia, clinical sexologist and internationally acclaimed expert on fetishism. One consists of people who think peeing is extremely pleasurable and enjoy the warmth and sensual experience of urination. The other is made up of those who regard peeing as a great taboo and who simply get off on the thrill of doing a "bad" thing.

"One group does it for purely hedonistic reasons . . . the tension, holding back and then release is a wonderful, delicious sense of 'ahhhh!' " says Brame, author of *Different Loving: The World of Sexual Dominance and Submission* (Villard, 1996), hailed as a landmark work on fetish subcultures. "The other group likes doing this wild thing, the extreme expression of something. They are thrill-seekers."

Brame says that as with most fetishes, there is a continuum of interest. Some people just like the feeling of a full bladder and then to release it, while others may go so far as to become urophiliacs (having a love of urine) or engaging in urolagnia (ingesting urine).

In the case of the woman in the shower it's likely she felt the shower was a neutral place to experiment with her lover because of the water and soap at hand to wash it away. Where she erred was in springing her leak on him without giving him notice. That amounted to a selfish act.

"It must have been a great shock to him. He might have felt she's some freak and can't control her bladder, or that she was just plain insulting him. To pee on someone without warning is really kind of sadistic. If she had said 'Honey, may I?' or 'This really turns me on,' it would have let him know the context was pleasure," Brame observes.

Although there is much to be said for spontaneity, it works only if both parties are on the same page, she notes.

"You don't get the right to do anything with anyone, only with someone who thinks it's fun to do. She foisted her own need upon him, and that could have been the straw that broke the camel's urinary tract."

? ? ?

"**Are** there any specific reasons for the lisp many gay men have when they talk?"

—DAN J., 32, white male

Readers Respond

"I'm sure some people won't like your question, but I know what you're saying. There definitely is a 'lilt' to the voices of many gay men. Sometimes it's a lisp, but more often it's an extra inflection (i.e., taking two syllables to say 'please'). I don't think there's a clear reason for it."

—W. CRANSTON, gay male

"Flamboyant speech seems to serve many purposes. For one, it is a way to mock those who mock us, sort of an in-your-face way of saying, 'Yeah, so what?' It can be a form of self-parody that can be a positive, witty way of expressing self-acceptance. Camp. It can be used to reveal ourselves or identify others. But for most I think it's copied because it's expressive, affirming and fun."

—DAVID, gay male

"I have traveled extensively in the United States, England, France, Germany, Australia and New Zealand. Most of my friends are gay. I have almost never heard the lilt or lisp that you refer to—certainly no more among gay men than among straights."

—STEVE K., 42, gay white male

"While there are still gay men who are effeminate (and proud of it), they are far fewer in number than just a few years ago. In the past, many gay men developed effeminate mannerisms as a defense mechanism, and as a way to revel in their 'differentness' once they accepted their sexuality. Gay men have always enjoyed crossing gender lines and questioning the need for the strict roles society forces on us. These days, as fewer gay men see themselves as outcasts, we act 'fabulous' only for fun, and turn it on or off to suit the occasion. So if you think the majority of gay men act effeminate, you're unaware of how many gays are around you every day!"

—MARK, 44, gay white male

Y?Check

Warren J. Blumenfeld, editor of the *International Journal of Sexuality and Gender Studies* (Kluwer Academic/Human Sciences Press) and coauthor of *Looking at Gay and Lesbian Life* (Beacon Press, 2001), has interviewed hundreds of gay men and lesbians for his research into gender, sexual orientation, and oppression.

Blumenfeld holds that people in mainstream culture tend to notice people who conform to stereotypes for a particular group and then see them as representing that entire group.

"We dismiss people who do not conform, seeing them as atypical or not even of that group," he says. "But if we see a man lisp who is gay, we will register that in our minds."

However, many stereotypes can have a kernel of truth to them, Blumenfeld adds, and in this case, lisping among gays can be traced back 100 or more years, to a time when "minstrelizing"—playing into the stereotypes of the dominant culture—was prevalent.

"Gays may have played into the lisp stereotype as a way of being accepted by straights, or even as a sign of internalized homophobia," he says. He adds that on the flipside, many gays today who have felt marginalized now see the inherent repression of mainstream gender-based roles and no longer feel compelled to stop lisping.

There is also the notion of "camp," not to be confused with minstrelizing, in which members of a group have fun with a stereotype about its members for the group's own benefit, to turn it into a positive aspect of their culture.

Ultimately, says Blumenfeld, who is gay, it is "probably not" true that more gays than straight men lisp, "and if it is, we don't care if it fulfills a stereotype, anyway."

? ? ?

"Some Irish guys I know talk about the 'Irish Curse'—a small penis. I also heard it mentioned in the movie <u>Good Will Hunting</u>. Is it true?"

—PETE, straight white male, 32

Readers Respond

"One thing you need to understand about Irish people is that we put ourselves down a lot, and the Irish Curse is one way we do it. I don't know if it's really got any truth to it. But yeah, I am below average. I have asked some pretty worldly female friends about their experiences, and most have said that Irish guys do tend to run small. I'm not threatened by this, so I guess I can admit that it is possible. I'd still rather be totally Irish than anything else."

—DAN R., 100 percent Irish male

"Oh how I laughed . . . No! It's untrue. Although I can, of course, only speak personally."

—AGRIVAINE

"I've definitely noticed that Irish guys tend to run a bit small. By this I mean 100 percent Irish guys only. I'm gay and have certainly seen a lot of erections in my life. Irish guys definitely fall toward the five-inch side of the spectrum, in my experience. My lover is Irish, so please don't take this as 'Irish bashing'; size is always nice, but it's not something to build a relationship on."

—TIM C., gay male

"It is not true. We Irish come in all sizes, just like any other race. I'm a little longer than average and 50 percent Irish."

—PATRICK, 52, gay male

"Is there an Irish Curse? I think so. I am 100 percent Irish and am slightly below average, like a few other Irish men I know. I've been at the heart of many penis jokes—'big like a house, hung like a mouse,' 'little dick' and, the worst for me personally, 'Mickey Mouse.' "

—MICKEY, Irish male

Y? Check

The Irish Curse has been the subject of mounting speculation the last few years. It's popular on Internet sites, and in 2002 the curse made a stage appearance as part of *The Penis Monologues,* a light production of Penn State University's student drama troupe.

But if a disgruntled Irishman wanted to blame his ancestors for his condition, he'd be hard up for scientific evidence supporting the claim.

It's not clear that anyone has documented a consistent deficit among the Irish or their American cousins, and in general, researchers have found considerable variation among men within all ethnic groups. However, several studies cited by the World Health Organization (WHO) in 1995 did indicate that, on average, men of African ancestry had slightly longer and wider penises than other groups, Caucasian men had medium measurements, and Asian men, on average, were smaller. The research was about more than bragging rights. The WHO considered ethnic differences when it set specifications for condoms in the 1990s. The nonprofit Family Health International supported studies to see whether men of different races would have less condom breakage and slippage using slightly different-size protection, but the results weren't very compelling.

Overall, men's measurements usually run between five and seven inches when erect, according to the 1990 Kinsey Institute New Report on Sex.

It's hard to say how famous the Irish Curse is. Hunter Wessells, chief of urology at Harborview Medical Center in Seattle, says he'd never heard of it and didn't recall any patient who considered it the root of his problem. Wessells, a University of Washington associate professor, was lead author of a 1997 article in *Contemporary Urology* called "Penile Size: What Is Normal?" that described a more insidious problem: Beginning in the 1990s, doctors faced swelling demand for enlargement surgery from normal-size men who thought they were inadequate.

"Why men believe they have a problem is intriguing and unknown," Wessells says, speculating that media images or pornography could give men false ideas about what's normal.

? ? ?

"**Even** my many gay and lesbian friends have a hard time answering this question: Why do gay men find drag queens and/or transsexuals attractive? If they are gay, doesn't that mean they prefer a person of the same sex?"

—RAVYNNE, 28, straight female

Readers Respond

"I'm gay and have absolutely no interest in transvestites and transsexuals. And, while I suppose I should be supportive of other gay people, I have found myself developing quite an intolerance for transvestites and their flamboyant ways."

—DOUG, 30, gay

"I have learned two things: 1) Being gay is not about sex, it is about who I am able to connect with on an intimate and emotional level. Sex is an expression of that connection. 2) It really is not the clothes that make the man!"

—STEVE N., 40, gay male

"Although I don't know why drag queens are a part of our queer culture (although they're certainly welcome), a friend of mine, a pre-operation transsexual who self-identifies as straight, said the main reason he and others in his situation are part of the gay community is that they were rejected by the mainstream community. Here in San Francisco, the so-called gay Mecca, my personal observation has been that the men you see in gay bars frequented by drag queens and transsexuals are usually straight. As for the attraction part, different strokes for different folks!"

—DANIEL, 27, gay white male

Y? Check

Take it from a drag diva: Gay men are not physically attracted to female impersonators. So says Lady Bunny, perhaps best known as the founder and Mistress of Ceremonies of Wigstock, New York's former Labor Day dragfest. She's performed for thousands over the last twenty years in nightclubs and at Wigstock.

Gay men essentially are attracted to gay men, and the last thing they want is someone who "minces around" in women's clothing, she says.

"Gay men put us on a pedestal because of our glamour or performances, but then they don't want to take us off that pedestal and screw us," Lady Bunny jokes. "Look at every gay personal ad—they all say 'no fats or femmes.' They want someone straight-acting."

That still doesn't answer why gay bars are filled with gay men watching and enjoying other gay men dressed up as women, however. For that answer, Lady Bunny points to gay males' love of and appreciation of sheer entertainment.

"If a drag queen is doing an accurate impersonation of, say, Whitney Houston or Dolly Parton or Judy Garland, then gays go for it. Drag is larger than life, glamorous and a theatrical device."

Beyond that, many gay men have an affinity for fashion and design and so naturally gravitate toward women's design over men's because of its fuller range of expression, she says.

This leads to perhaps the deeper reason for drag's popularity: its ability to transcend society's rules about what's acceptable or not—an attribute with high appeal to gay males, many of whom suffer or have suffered oppression almost daily.

"To see someone exaggerate feminine qualities, it is kind of liberating," Lady Bunny says. "Gay men spend so much of their time trying to make themselves more masculine to fit into society or to be more desirable in their own society. It's somewhat freeing to see someone who is completely flouting society's desires."

So with effeminate gay men and drag queens at the bottom of the totem pole when it comes to the gay dating scene, what's a diva to do?

"Almost exclusively I'm hit on by straight-identifying men," Lady Bunny says. "If you are the kind of straight guy whose main sexual focus is to put your dick into a hole and you don't care what that hole is because your sexual satisfaction is centered on your dick, then you will go with a drag queen who will either fellate you or get screwed by you. If, on the other hand, you are into the vagina, the smell of it, the taste of it, then you won't be satisfied with a drag queen or a transvestite."

? ? ?

"Regarding sexual intercourse: Why do some gay people prefer being the socket, and others the plug?"

—NEIL, male

Readers Respond

"There could be a couple of reasons. A 'bottom' (or socket as you say) could prefer stimulation of the prostate gland over stimulation of the penis to achieve orgasm. Or it could be a matter of size: The bottom's penis may be too small to stimulate another's prostate, or too big for comfortable, pain-free penetration of the anus. Most gay couples I know tend to go either way. I only have one friend who is solely bottom, because he has only a three-inch erection and can achieve a better orgasm through stimulation of his prostate."

—MIKE, 42, gay white male

"The large majority of gay people are open to all aspects of a same-sex physical liaison. While being the 'plug' has benefits that most straight men can also relate to, being the 'socket' provides direct prostate stimulation, which can provide intense orgasms. Additionally, some people have an innate desire to please their partner more so than having to 'be pleased' themselves. This is common in both straight and gay sex, but is more definable in gay anal sex."

—STEPHEN, 37, gay male

"For each man it's different, and many redefine themselves many times in their lives. The important thing is to not feel confined by a label, and to do what you feel comfortable doing."

—JOSH, 22, Jewish gay male

"It may depend on the day, the partner and the alignment of the stars. And, remember, just being gay does not necessarily mean liking anal sex. I know a gay man who says anal sex is far better in concept than execution. The other thing is that the roles get tied up with perceptions of gender. At different times and places, you aren't 'really' gay if nobody sticks their penis into any part of your body. Weird. The big thing is to be open to learning about what *you* like, and with whom. Enjoying anal sex can take a bit of learning, and a lot of trust and patience (and always, always, a condom)."

—ANDY, 37, gay white male

"Even if a guy acts in ways that might convince you he's a top or bottom, it wouldn't be surprising if that turned out not to be accurate. After all, if you've got a ticket to the fun park, why limit yourself to just one type of ride?"

—BEN S., 31, gay white male

Y? Check

Popular images of feminine-acting "bottoms" and macho "tops" in the gay community generally don't hold up to scrutiny, according to Barry Adam, a sociologist who interviewed gay men in Ontario, Canada, for a lengthy sexuality study.

"Men who appear to be effeminate may very well be tops, and men who are masculine may be bottoms," says Adam, a professor at the University of Windsor in Ontario, Canada.

His research and that of others suggests as much at 80 percent of gay men in North America would classify themselves as "versatile"—i.e., both "givers" and "receivers." Adam said that's probably a result of national egalitarian values and a consensus that developed inside gay culture during the past half-century. For example, men who are top-only can face resentment for acting as though they're better than their partners, he says.

But the rules aren't the same worldwide. Although men in Europe and Australia are also likely to be versatile, Adam says research in South America has found more men who took just one role.

There are also gay men, maybe a tenth of those in some surveys, who don't practice anal sex at all. Adam says men who are relatively new to gay life are most likely to fall into that category.

? ? ?

"**Is** it true that black men do not like to perform oral sex on women?"

—SHANNON, female

Readers Respond

"I love to. However, when I was younger, most black men at least said they wouldn't do it. That may have had something to do with a view that whites would do anything sexually, so not doing so was a rejection of something 'dirty' that whites do."

—WAYNE C., 41, black male

"It can be scary downtown . . . if you don't have a map. We aren't taught about women's bodies by the people who should know better—their owners themselves—and many of us grow up believing women are naturally unclean because of various reproductive myths and half-truths that come from clinical ignorance borne of shame or the idea of 'being proper.' No one goes there with us verbally, so we don't go there physically."

—RANDY, 28, black male

"Can't speak for all brothas, but for me, it's the first thing on my mind."

—ORONDE, 28, black male

"I attend a predominantly black school, and many of the black males I know brag about performing oral sex. Maybe it's just a difference in age—it seems high school kids will do just about anything."

—MONICA, 17, black female

"I enjoy giving and receiving. For me, the main issue is hygiene. I heard it put well once on one of those dating TV shows: The man (who wasn't black) told his date: 'I'm a diver. And as long as the water is clear, I can stay down until my air runs out.' I'm with him."

—ELLIOTT, 37, black male

"Many black men and women like to put each other down a great deal as far as sex and relationships go. I feel this is part of the problem. If a black man is prone to putting down black women a lot, they will probably never admit to performing oral sex on a black woman because she 'doesn't deserve it.' "

—R., 22, black female

"Inhibitions still prevail, and many black women and men my age still will not admit to giving oral sex. I still have vivid memories of my white cheerleader friends demonstrating how to give oral sex to a guy and white guys offering us oral sex while doing similar demonstrations."

—YVETTE, 45, black female

Y? Check

Black men and women indeed "lag behind when it comes to oral sex," says counselor and relationship expert Dr. Rosie Milligan, who has spent fourteen years researching black sexuality. Among books she has written and published through her company, Milligan Books, in 1994 are *Satisfying the Black Man Sexually* and *Satisfying the Black Woman Sexually.*

She points to the textbook *Understanding Human Sexuality* by Janet Shibley Hyde and John D. Delamater, in which it is reported that the percentage of those performing oral sex by ethnic group are: white men—81 percent; white women—75 percent; Hispanic men—71 percent; Hispanic women—60 percent; black men—51 percent; and black women—34 percent.

"Blacks have not been as sexually free in comparison to other races, because of their history of rape and forced sex during slavery," Milligan says. "Black men were made to have sex with black women not for love or enjoyment, but to produce work hands for his master. If one would revisit history and the living conditions of blacks who were brought here as slaves, then you could understand why blacks' sexual appetites are different."

In fact, under the conditions in which many lived, oral sex was likely a repulsive proposition, she notes.

"Blacks did not live in homes with running water. As a result, people bathed once a week. Many would refer to the male and female genitals as being nasty. After working the fields from sun-up to sun-down, their bodies would be sweaty, musty and dirty."

Even as recently as the past decade, oral sex was portrayed as a "white thing."

"When watching movies, white folk made love, while blacks just fucked. There was no caressing or petting shown between blacks. There was no intimacy and foreplay. You saw whites licking, kissing and sucking, etc. When blacks made such a request or admitted to performing oral sex, other blacks would accuse them of acting white," Milligan says.

According to her research, black men still aren't too big on giving oral sex.

"Most black men surveyed enjoy having oral sex performed on them, but were least likely to perform it on their sexual partners," she says. "While black women may perform oral sex on multiple partners, a black man wants the assurance that he is the only one that she is letting lick the bowl, and that he is the only man that she performs oral sex with."

? ? ?

"**Why** do lesbians tend to be so masculine?"

—CHARLYNN O., female

R e a d e r s R e s p o n d

"People always ask me and my girlfriend which of us is the boy. Argh! If we wanted to be with a boy, we'd be with one. They are not that hard to come by. No matter how butch or femme a woman is, she's still a woman, and that's the important thing. So what if she looks masculine? She has the perspective of having lived life as a woman, and that makes all the difference. Who knows better how to please a woman (sexually, emotionally and otherwise) but another woman?"

—SHERRY, 27, lesbian

"I am a woman who prefers women. I also wear dresses and shave my legs and have long hair and paint my fingernails. I have all the body parts a straight female has, and I wear heels on occasion."

—T., lesbian

"I am a gay, 35-year-old woman who has been out more than 15 years. I am in a relationship not based on how feminine I am or how butch my wife is. It is wonderful not to feel pigeon-holed. She is more athletic, but I am more tool-oriented; she does not wear feminine clothes, yet she is not butch. I like to wear dresses, but I'm the one outside with the chainsaw cutting firewood. There is no masculine or feminine between us. That is an antiquated condition on its way out. There will always be very butch women, and they will be beautiful in their own way, celebrating their womanhood (not femininity) in their own way. There will be very effeminate men celebrating their manhood (not machismo) in their own way."

—C. FOSTER, 35, lesbian

"All the lesbians I know express their preferences in appearance and behavior without regard to what some consider masculine and feminine. Lesbians like women and are comfortable conducting themselves without regard to gender roles and constraints."

—CHERYL H., lesbian

Y? Check

Numerous studies have been conducted in recent decades measuring the masculinity and femininity of lesbians, says J. Michael Bailey, associate professor of psychology at Northwestern University and a leading authority on sexual orientation and gender identity.

"The short answer is . . . yes, on average, lesbians are more masculine than straight females," he says. Writing for the textbook *Clinical, Developmental, and Policy Issues Facing Lesbians, Gay Males, and Bisexuals* (Harcourt Brace, 1995), Bailey reports that in a review of sixteen studies in which lesbians and heterosexual women recalled their childhood behavior, approximately 80 percent of lesbians were more masculine than the typical straight woman.

Meanwhile, Bailey says, his own research and that of others offers some validity to notions that lesbians tend to have more masculine interests than straight females, as well as a more masculine gait to their walk. They also tend to sport shorter haircuts than straight females, have less interest in fashion than heterosexual women, and have more interest in occupations stereotypically associated with males.

Such findings have not been greeted with great enthusiasm in the gay community, he notes in the textbook. Also contentious, Bailey says, is his hypothesis that hormonal factors that contribute to a "masculinizing of the brain" are at the root of butchness in lesbians. Though some research has supported this idea, conclusive results have yet to be achieved, he adds.

Other sex and gender researchers also take exception to the notion that lesbians are more "butch" than straight females. Rhoda Unger, a Women's Studies Scholar at Brandeis University who specializes in social psychology as it relates to women and gender, believes that such misconceptions are fostered because many people think they can "spot" a lesbian by dress or appearance. However, "Most lesbians look just like other women," she writes in *Women and Gender: A Feminist Psychology* (McGraw-Hill, 1992), which she coauthored. "The 'butch' stereotype is probably related to the belief, common among heterosexuals, that lesbians are women who want to be men."

? ? ?

"What is the connection the gay community (particularly gay men) has to the movie <u>The Wizard of Oz</u>?"

—JODI, 26

Readers Respond

"I believe the answer lies in the plot: A young person, persecuted for her affections, seeks to find a place where she can be accepted and explore herself—but once discovered, longs for the simplicity of her former life, only to find that everything she sought was in her heart all along. It mirrors the coming-out experience for many gay men, myself included, who felt uncomfortable in their family life and searched for meaning in the big, wide world, ultimately to return to the comfort and nurturing of a 'family' environment (frequently a close circle of friends or a significant relationship)."

—DOUG L., 35, gay white male

"The main reason has to be the overall camp quality of the movie. And many gay men recognize and appreciate good camp. Just thinking about the house falling down on the Wicked Witch and Dorothy getting the ruby slippers, or the scene with the poppy fields (think drugs) brings a wry smile to my face."

—TONY, 36, gay black male

"The Stonewall Rebellion, the last Sunday in June 1969, where drag queens and other gay people revolted against police repression at the Stonewall Inn in Greenwich Village, coincided with the death of Judy Garland, who, of course, starred in *The Wizard of Oz*. Some gay historians suggest that grief over Garland's death (she was already a gay icon) provided the emotional rage needed to stand up against years of abuse by corrupt New York City cops. The Stonewall Rebellion is considered the starting point of the modern gay rights movement and is why Gay Pride Day occurs (or at least is supposed to occur) on the last Sunday of every June."

—CHUCK, gay male

Y?Check

Dorothy and her friends from Oz have an iconic status in gay culture that's easier to see than explain. Businesses from clothing shops to travel agencies use Oz references in their names to show they target gay clientele. Kansas farm girl costumes have become stock items in gay pride parades. And whether it was intended or not, the rainbow flag's introduction as a community symbol in the 1970s gave "over the rainbow" a new meaning for many Americans.

But under all the layers of pop culture, the original attraction to *The Wizard of Oz* might just be its story, says Dee Michel, a fan who is researching a book about the connection between Oz and the gay community. After more than ninety detailed interviews of gay Oz enthusiasts, Michel says fans routinely say they loved the story as small children, long before they would express any sexual orientation. Many of them liked fantasy in general and were also apt to enjoy movies like *Star Wars* that offered sheer escapism.

But Oz, both in the century-old book and the 1939 movie, has elements Michel thinks hold extra meaning for gay men. Dorothy's friends—the scarecrow, tin man, and cowardly lion— are quirky, offbeat souls who don't fit male stereotypes but still find acceptance.

"They're certainly not your typical macho, John Wayne, football-player types," said Michel, who was introduced to the story in childhood by his father, who was also gay. The trip to find the wizard is really a journey of self-discovery, started because Dorothy had problems at home, and Michel says that could also resonate with gay fans.

Conjecture that Judy Garland was the reason for the Oz phenomenon took a beating in Michel's surveys. When he asked Oz fans to name their other favorite movies, only a handful mentioned anything else starring her.

It's hard to say exactly how long Dorothy's journey has been a fixture in gay culture. There's documentation dating to the 1970s, but reliable history about gay culture before then is limited, says Michel, who taught library science at the University of Wisconsin– Madison and is now a consultant in western Massachusetts.

There are claims that gay men in the 1950s were invoking the story by describing themselves as "a friend of Dorothy," but there have been alternative explanations offered. When Michel lectured about gay men and Oz at an International Wizard of Oz Club conference marking the book's centennial in 2000, it was said to be the first time the club formally addressed the subject.

? ? ?

"**Why** is it homophobic to believe there are some situations in which heterosexuals have a right to insist gays or lesbians be excluded? It is my belief that homosexuality is an unfortunate aberration like other genetic disabilities. I embrace the right of out gay people to compete in the marketplace, with two or three exceptions, e.g., military basic training and the teaching profession up through middle school. I have worked for and respected a gay boss, and I have served on the boards of several arts organizations and count a number of gay individuals among my coterie of friends."

-J.G., 60, straight male

Readers Respond

"Why, what a fortunate coterie of gay friends you have! They have in you a friend with such affection, respect and understanding for them, yet from whose every pore seeps contempt and fear. You don't need to ask questions about gay people, you need to ask questions about friendship."

—MAX M., gay male

"Why should I think that I, a grown, educated woman who pays taxes, loves and lives, should be excluded from anything? Because a straight 60-year-old thinks I should? It's great you can work alongside gays, but I'd hate to have you as a boss or parent."

—K.R., lesbian

"We are talking about gay people here, not pedophiles, which I trust you realize are two different things."

—HERO, female

"Who decides which genetic traits are acceptable and which are not? I can't think of a situation in which the exclusion of gays would be anything other than homophobic, except perhaps for a straight orgy! In any other place, one's behavior in the bedroom has no bearing on other activities and, therefore, exclusion is homophobic, pure and simple."

—MARK, gay male

"You feign love of all people, including gays, but believe it is for our own good—as well as society's—that we be socially constrained in ways that heterosexuals are not. I would rather be perceived as a criminal than to win membership in your kind of society."

—EZEKIEL K., 47, gay male

Y?Check

The term "homophobia" is thrown around loosely these days, when most of the time what people really mean is "anti-gay bias," says Sean Cahill, director of the Policy Institute for the National Gay and Lesbian Task Force, a Washington, D.C.–based organization that works for gay rights.

"People who oppose non-discrimination laws for gay people, or same-sex marriage, or anti-bias initiatives in schools, are they all homophobic? I think most are not," Cahill says. "I think they are promoting policy that is anti-gay, but if you are opposed to legal equality for gay people, that doesn't necessarily mean you have a psychological hang-up."

Taken literally, true phobias originate from irrational fear and anxiety. Indeed, in a much-discussed study released in 2002, researchers at the University of Arkansas found that homophobia was not an actual phobia, but a condition arising from feelings of disgust or concern of contamination. In surveys completed by 138 participants, psychology professor Jeff Lohr and graduate students Bunmi Olatunji and Suzanne Meunier found a social and attitudinal basis for negative attitudes about homosexuals, not a psychopathological one.

Olatunji, lead author of the study, suggested that antigay hostility was a prejudicial attitude akin to racism; he reported that feedback he received suggested "homonegativism" might be a more accurate term.

To Cahill, gay rights opponents aren't necessarily irrational or illogical—just wrong. "They are putting their personal prejudice into public policy. It's not socially acceptable to do that with other demographic groups, but it's still acceptable with gays."

To suggest that gays should not teach children, for example, is "a pretty degrading and offensive way of thinking," he says.

"A lot of us are educators, a lot of us are in social services. You're saying we're not allowed to do this? That's two million jobs right there. Where do you draw the line? What about the ticket taker at the movie theater? They come into contact with teens. And what are we going to do with the kids of millions of gay parents? Put them in foster care?"

Still, those who oppose gay rights needn't be branded with such a highly charged word as "homophobic," Cahill notes.

"Gays don't want to be pathologized; we succeeded in getting the American Psychological Association to stop classifying homosexuality as a mental disorder, and we shouldn't classify people who disagree as having a mental disorder, either," he says. "They are wrong, and it's important to debate them to change their views, but we need to treat them respectfully."

? ? ?

"I'm going to college soon and was curious about how hard it is to find time to masturbate while living with a roommate. Also, is it common for this topic to be up for discussion between roommates? I even heard some roommates do it together. Is this true?"

—MIKE, 18, white male

Readers Respond

"Roommates don't share every minute of every day together. You'll have time to yourself. I think it would be unusual for roommates to discuss it, and even rarer to do it together—but anything's possible."

—A., 35, male

"My only advice is, do not wait until you think your roommate is asleep and then do it in your bunk. Many guys got the reputation of creating a 'three-minute earthquake' in their bunkbed. It is not a reputation you want."

—JASON B., 26, white male

"Your roommate will have the same urges as you, so just speak with him. I mean, if you two become really good friends, maybe you can just start to give blowjobs to each other. The guys across the hall from me used to do that all the time, and we never thought of them as being different or gay or anything. Just don't swallow. That would make you gay."

—MALIK R., male

"My sophomore year, one night I was doing it when I noticed my roommate had pulled away his sheets and was masturbating, too. I pulled my sheets back and proceeded, and within minutes we both climaxed. Not a word was ever said between us, but that went on almost every night from that point forward. Junior year, another college and another roommate. It was the same story—until about mid-November, when he noticed me doing it one night and came over and laid down next to me and started up. We eventually ended up giving each other hand jobs and discussing techniques. Nothing beyond that, though. I look back on that with no remorse or guilt whatsoever."

—MIKE, 41, white male

"I masturbate. A lot. I live in a dorm room with one other person, and we have the public bathroom thing. When I first got here, that was a problem for me. Well, my roommate now knows that I do it. I admit it openly to people most of the time (it actually turns a lot of guys' cranks, which is good for me). It's really easy to hide it when you don't have to move all that much. I wouldn't suggest using a vibrator, though. It's a little hard to convince a roommate that you're brushing your teeth with an electric toothbrush at 10 P.M."

—JAKKI, 18, straight white female

Y? Check

Up there somewhere on the shelf of college-life angst rests this question, perhaps not as important as worrying about passing finals, but looming nonetheless. To this, licensed social worker Carleton Kendrick says, "Get thee to the shower, young man."

"Even in an *Animal House*-like dormitory, this is the one place you can find at least temporary solace," he said.

But rest assured, there will be time alone, when roommates' schedules have them going different directions.

"Eventually, he'll find the comings and goings of his roommates, no pun intended," says Kendrick, a longtime therapist and coauthor of *Take Out Your Nose Ring, Honey, We're Going to Grandma's: Hanging In, Holding On and Letting Go of Your Teen* (Unlimited Publishing, 2003).

"My thought would be at the very least until he finds out the schedules, hit the showers—and try not to get too shriveled up," Kendrick says.

"When I was in college, I knew a couple of kids who would just say, 'Look, I'm going to jerk off—give me 15 minutes,' " he said.

For the not-so-direct?

"Chances are no one would think untoward of him if he just kind of said, "If I'm in the room and have a necktie over the doorknob, I don't wish to be disturbed," Kendrick says.

Fortunately, there's a growing openness about discussing self-pleasure these days.

"Whether it's to relieve stress or to make sure you last longer with your girlfriend in two hours, or just for plain hedonistic pleasure, I say verily, verily," Kendrick says.

? ? ?

"**Why** do so many straight people think gays and lesbians will sleep with anyone breathing?"

—SEX-LESS, 45, white lesbian

Readers Respond

"I happen to believe that gays, generally speaking, are promiscuous. This is not to say some aren't as committed as traditional couples, but on the whole that commitment is lacking. I base this on a number of things, not least of which is the homosexual assertion that having multiple sexual partners is a defining parameter of that lifestyle. Studies on AIDS almost always mention in passing that multiple sex partners is the rule rather than the exception. AIDS would not be an epidemic if gays weren't as promiscuous as they are."

—NORM, 50, straight white male

"The vast majority of AIDS cases worldwide are the result of transmission via heterosexual sex. As for the promiscuity issue, single straight people (and an extremely high percentage of married straight men) tend to sleep around quite a lot."

—FRANK, 23, gay white male

"Studies show men in general are more promiscuous than women. So men having relationships with men have more freedom."

—N. SMITH, 44, white lesbian

"There are more gay people in the non-openly-gay/non-news-taped neighborhoods than in the gay-ghettos, and they aren't on the news. They've got houses, play the organ at the Catholic church, work together around the house, volunteer at school, mow the yard with their partner, and don't sleep around."

—PATRICK S., 24, gay white male, Catholic

"It is my experience that men in general are more promiscuous than women, especially men in their late teens and early 20s. But as these men, straight and gay, grow older and develop friendships, achieving that next orgasm isn't as important as it once was. It isn't a gay or straight thing. It is a youth and sexual freedom thing. Period."

—T., 37, gay male

"*Cheers* was in the Nielsen Top 10 for nine years. The main character, Sam, slept with hundreds of women. Watchers thought of it as cute and funny. Wilt Chamberlain claimed to have slept with 10,000 women. Rather than question his morals, the public mostly questioned whether he was lying. We have words for heterosexual men who have many female sex partners: player, stud, stallion, ladies' man, Romeo, Casanova. Does this mean all heterosexuals are promiscuous?"

—CRAIG, 35, gay male

Y ? C heck

Gay men in long-term romances might put less emphasis on monogamy on average than their straight counterparts, according to research by Barry Adam, a sociologist at the University of Windsor in Ontario, Canada.

Adam interviewed gay men in relationships of a year or more and found the rules for exclusivity were much more individualized than those many straight couples follow. Only about a quarter of the gay men were monogamous, and the others had a wide variety of arrangements suited to their relationship. Some were okay with outside flings if they were kept secret, but others would only consider pursuing another man if they could share him with their partner.

"The short answer is there's a wide diversity," Adam says, adding that a lot of couples develop their rules when they move in together. Another finding: Men who were younger or had less gay experience, or had immigrated from Latino or Asian cultures, were more likely to support monogamy.

Adam says he thinks many men start out thinking about their relationships the way straight couples do and gradually develop their own boundaries as they gain experience.

? ? ?

"At my job we have a person who is in the process of undergoing a sex change from man to woman. How should I identify and address this person, as a man or a woman—i.e., ex-him, her, Mr., Ms.?"

—GEORGE

Readers Respond

"The most polite way to address the person in transition is by the gender in which they present themselves, i.e., a male becoming a woman would be addressed with feminine pronouns, and a female becoming a male would be addressed with masculine pronouns—unless of course they direct differently."

—JENNIFER D., 49, bisexual white female

"As a woman! It is really not a question of sexual orientation—she may like girls or boys—but of gender identity. She sees herself as a woman deeply enough to go through this very hard process. Saying 'she' (and 'Ms.' is always safe) is, even if hard at first, a real kindness, and also very appropriate."

—JESSICA

"I've only just realized to what extent it is that other behavior, not just courtesy titles, makes us feel respected. The appropriate eye contact, touches, kindnesses, inclusion in activities, social invitations, etc. make as much difference as the way we are addressed. Remember that what you are seeing is not a 'man dressed as a woman,' but a woman. Her body might not fit your image of a female, especially with the inevitable tricks that your memory will play on you, but she is a woman."

—DAVID W.

"Though I'm not transgendered (I'm just not feeling comfortable with any gender), I will say that all transgendered people I have known personally, and there are some 20 of them, have preferred to be called by their 'emotional' gender."

—KAKRI, 38, white female

Y? Check

A sex change doesn't have to be a gender-bender for anyone involved, as long as some proper advance work is done, says Jennifer Finney Boylan, cochair of the English Department at Colby College in Maine, who described her own change in the memoir *She's Not There: A Life in Two Genders* (Broadway Books, 2003).

Such a change inspires complex etiquette issues simply because, in time, it will become obvious to everyone from dear friends and family to the most casual acquaintances. They don't all need the same level of information, but the person going through gender transition can expect to face questions in every sphere of his or her life.

At work, that person has a responsibility for managing the transition with professionalism and competence, says Boylan.

Those undergoing a change should choose a time to go public, she says. Before doing so, he or she should communicate with immediate supervisors at work and with the employer's human resources director. Supervisors might choose to talk to those who work closely with the person undergoing transition.

"Then a letter ought to go out to everyone, explaining in open, optimistic, professional terms what the transition will entail," Boylan says.

Being open about the change makes rules for names and pronouns pretty simple, she notes.

"Before the transition is public, the person ought to be referred to by their old name and pronoun. After coming out, the person ought to be referred to by the new one," Boylan says. "People ought to work very hard to make sure there are not slip-ups; but for a while, slip-ups ought to be forgiven."

Coworkers are going to have questions, and the person going through transition should have answers ready for reasonable inquiries, Boylan says. She says it's a good idea to have books available for people with sincere interest. Volumes such as *True Selves* (Jossey-

Bass, 1996, by Mildred Brown and Chloe Rounsley), a guide to transsexualism for families, friends, and coworkers, could help put some questions to rest.

The subject seems to be raising continuing questions for business administrators as well. The Society for Human Resource Management posted a white paper on managing gender transition on its website, and references to the issue have appeared elsewhere in HR publications.

? ? ?

"**Why** does it seem that so many gay males are involved in theater, dance or the arts? When younger, I always believed this was a horrible stereotype, which I still essentially believe."

—BROADWAY BOUND, 15, gay male

Readers Respond

"A horrible stereotype to realize that homosexuality and artistic gifts are linked? I wouldn't call it that. I would say you are simply noticing reality. More than 90 percent of church organists are gay. It's not a stereotype, it's just that these things are linked. Straight men are out there building it, and we are out there designing and decorating it! I'm not offended to learn that I'm sensitive, artistic, musical, spiritual and homosexual. I'm proud of it."

—JIM, gay male

"Jim, that's a crock. I am out there building the churches also, and so are a lot of my gay friends, and we love it. I am not a decorator, dancer or designer. Not all, or even most, gay men are artistic. I hate those stereotypes."

—KYLE, 30, gay black male

"Success in the arts is very hard to come by. That many gay people succeed is a testimony to their talent, persistence, endurance and guts.

Who wouldn't want a career in theater instead of accounting? Or to be a world-famous dancer instead of an anonymous engineer? Who wouldn't want the excitement of performing to cheering crowds instead of a dull, nine-to-five job in front of a computer? This 'stereotype' of gays arises from one simple thing: pure, unadulterated envy by the untalented."

—MARK

Y? Check

No, not all gay men are drama queens—literally or figuratively—says John M. Clum, whose books on homosexuality and the theater include *Acting Gay* (Columbia University Press, 1992), regarded as a classic in the field, and *Something for the Boys* (St. Martin's Press, 1999).

There has been commentary for decades about the number of gay men in the arts, particularly in musical theater. During the "Red Scare" of the 1950s, someone coined the word "Homintern" (short for "Homosexual International") to describe a gay cabal that supposedly pulled the strings behind America's entertainment industry. Publicity about the sex lives of luminaries from Cole Porter to Stephen Sondheim and Harvey Fierstein helped seal the image that gay men found a haven in entertainment.

But that idea has lost touch with the times, notes Clum.

"Now, actually, you might find more gay men in law and business school than conservatories," says Clum, chairman of theater studies at Duke University in North Carolina. "One gay student recently remarked to me that there was a larger proportion of gay men in fraternities than in arts organizations at the school at which I teach. This would not have been the case even 10 years ago."

? ? ?

"Do lesbians enjoy looking at nude, pornographic pictures of women as much as men do?"

—DON B.

Readers Respond

"As a gay female, I enjoy looking at photos of nude women. But many of my gay friends do not. In fact, it seems almost taboo in the gay female community to express an affinity for porn. I believe it has a lot to do with a perception of political correctness being incongruent with enjoying nude pictures of women. Some studies suggest porn is oppressive to women, and although I agree that some venues of illicit porn do oppress, not all nudity does. I enjoy *Playboy* and *Hustler,* but some of the themes disturb me, like portrayal of supposedly very young girls, bondage, rape and submission. But I believe most lesbians would agree that the depiction of a beautiful nude woman is a wonderful vision to behold."

—L.H., 35, gay female

"I am a bisexual woman who gets very turned on by watching pornography. It is one of the traits my boyfriend likes about me. I get more turned on by the lesbian than heterosexual scenes. I think it is because women know what women like, so they understand more of what they are doing and it is usually not as harsh-looking as the heterosexual sex in porns."

—27-year-old, just realizing I'm bi

"I will not look away from a nude picture of a woman, because I think women have beautiful bodies. I also look at nudes to critique a body, just as a lot of others do ('Nice legs! Whoa, is that a pimple on her buttock?') The only time I look at porn is if someone else is looking at it while I'm around. I don't watch for long, but when I do, I'm usually clowning the sex scenes—'Ha ha wow, that girl looks mighty uncomfortable.' I never get sexual pleasure out of looking at pornography, but I usually do get a good laugh."

—CHRISSY, 21, lesbian

Y? Check

Plenty of lesbians occasionally leaf through "dirty" magazines—and not just for the articles, says Heather Findlay, editor-in-chief of *On Our Backs,* a bimonthly magazine produced by and for lesbians, with an estimated readership of 45,000.

And although it's totally overshadowed by publishing behemoths such as *Playboy* and *Penthouse,* there is a lesbian porn industry in America, she adds. In addition to *On Our Backs,* there are also calendars and pictorial books aimed at lesbians, as well as a variety of lesbian erotic writing.

"Anybody who is a sexual person, whether they're gay or straight, enjoys beautiful nudity," says Findlay. Her forty-eight-page magazine usually has three main pictorials—two showing two or more women engaging in various graphic sex acts, and one about a single woman. Counting other art scattered through the pages, there are usually ten to fifteen women pictured per issue.

But this isn't your father's porn magazine, and the models make that pretty obvious.

"My readers like to see themselves reflected in the photographs," Findlay says, noting that women in *On Our Backs* are more likely to have short hair and short nails, and that large-bodied and minority women are also more common than in most men's magazines.

What you won't see is rows of models with boob jobs, long nails, and lots of blond hair, which Findlay says just looks too much like stereotyped male porn. (Although to be fair, she says, some customers also buy men's magazines.)

One of the thorniest challenges for lesbian porn over the years has been a chilly, sometimes hostile reaction from many feminists. It's been banned from some lesbian feminist bookstores, and some critics have trashed it in the same manner they denounce men's porn.

The ridicule has softened with time, but it has never vanished. Findlay says erotic publications help lesbians address their sexuality and are too important to be shunned.

"They're part of our liberation," she says. "The proper response to some of the uglier aspects of pornography was not to censor it, but to do it ourselves . . . and to make it right."

> ? ? ?

"**Is** coming out still frightening for homosexuals? It seems that it wouldn't be, with so many people publicly out."

—R.J., white, straight

Readers Respond

"Since I came out when I was 18, I've noticed more and more people coming out, too. For me, it wasn't nearly as frightening as I thought it would be. When I told my family about my homosexuality, they were like 'And . . .?' None of them love me any less for who I am. I am still a little scared to tell my father. I almost did once, but my mother talked me out of it."

—ANDREW V., 32, gay male

"As a member of a youth group that serves gay, lesbian, bisexual and transgender youth in the Atlanta area, I can tell you that coming out is definitely still a very scary experience for a lot of young people. Usually it's not as hard when the person you are coming out to is younger, but depending on the attitudes of the person and the relationship that existed beforehand, even then, coming out can be seriously nerve-wracking and can cause major problems."

—WENDY D., 23, white, bisexual

"Teenagers will lock themselves in their rooms if they have a pimple. Drill holes into tender flesh just to fit in. Alienate their family to avoid being made fun of by their friends. And those are the straight ones. When sexuality rears its horny head and a teenager starts to realize he or she is different from other people, the first impulse is to hide. It doesn't matter that people on TV are gay—they are not your friends. It doesn't matter if there are other gay people in your school—they just help take the heat off you. Fit in, fit in, fit in is the drumbeat. Coming out is a lifelong process of explaining to everyone you meet that you do not have a wife at home cooking your dinner, don't appreciate the ass on that woman, and like watching football not because you care who wins but because you like to see guys touching and groping and pawing each other (all right, maybe that last one is just me)."

—CHARLES B., 47, gay male

Y? Check

Coming out is still no picnic.

So says Tedd Adams, a longtime volunteer facilitator for the Oklahoma Rainbow Young Adult Network (ORYAN), a state-sponsored gay youth support group.

It's important to understand that coming out is a process, and one that doesn't necessarily include coming out to everyone at the same time, he says. It's not at all uncommon for someone to be out to everyone except family or coworkers.

What drives these exceptions is fear, he notes.

"Sadly, these fears are often well-founded. Even though public acceptance is on the rise, there are still countless individual stories, most of which we never hear about, but some, such as the Matthew Shepard murder, which garner national attention."

For these reasons, many people stay in the closet, Adams says.

"They fear violence; they fear rejection by parents, friends and coworkers, and they fear losing property, housing or jobs."

In addition, "Gay kids are sent tacit messages nearly daily, by their families, teachers and friends, that it's not okay to be gay. In any school, anti-gay slurs are passed around the halls like candy at Halloween, yet rare is the teacher who will stand up and protest such language. Similarly, in the workforce, anti-gay bias persists and can lead to harassment or stalled career growth."

The tide is turning, however, Adams reports: According to the Human Rights Campaign, a national organization working for gay, lesbian, bisexual, and transgender equal rights, more than half of Fortune 500 companies now offer a nondiscrimination policy that includes sexual orientation, and thousands of private companies do the same.

Public acknowledgment by some celebrities of their homosexuality has helped, too, Adams says.

"In the last decade, we have seen numerous celebrities come out of the closet and not only keep their career intact, but actually flourish," he says. "Melissa Etheridge, Elton John and Rosie O'Donnell have enjoyed continued success even after coming out."

As well, several important court rulings have helped allay the fear of coming out, Adams says, including the U.S. Supreme Court's ruling that effectively decriminalized homosexual activity in all states.

"Overall, what seems to be driving the improved 'safety factor' for coming out is a heightened awareness . . . with increased public dialogue and ready access to information via television and the Internet, it's impossible to deny the ubiquity of gay, lesbian and bisexual people."

? ? ?

"**I'm** a straight female but constantly find myself becoming desperately attracted to gay men, a.k.a. a 'fag-hag.' How does this make homosexual males feel?"

—JENNIFER E., 20, straight female

Readers Respond

"When your attraction is serious (you want to get into a relationship, etc.), it can be pretty uncomfortable. Even when a night out turns into a date, it gets pretty touchy. Recently I went out with a female friend, and it turned into a date. I'm not out to her, and the situation was pretty awkward for me. I wouldn't call your attraction to gay men annoying. As you probably already know, most gay men are pretty understanding. By the way, there's no problem being a fag hag. It actually means you're a close female friend and supporter."

—JASON, gay male

"How I as a gay man feel with it depends—as most attractions do—on how you act on it. If I get pressed, it feels like harassment, and the 'ick factor' goes up proportionately to how hard she's working it. So don't. I find I back off from even hugging straight women if I feel like they've got a hubba-hubba agenda."

—MAX M., gay male

Y? Check

The "fag-hag/gay male" social relationship is "very symbiotic and should be of no surprise to anyone," says Jeffery Lensman, a forty-year-old gay male active in Unity Utah, a gay/lesbian/transgender political support group.

Women with a "straight eye for the queer guy" usually are attracted to the attention they receive from a gay man, who in these cases is usually a more effeminate type as opposed to "your macho-gay-leather-man-type of dude," Lensman says. On the flip side, the gay man enjoys the platonic relationship with these women because they can engage in "girl talk" (they share a common interest in men, after all).

"It can be a very enjoyable social exchange for both parties," says Lensman.

However, such pairings can have a potentially damaging outcome after a period of time, he notes.

"I have seen it happen many times where the woman feels compelled to let the guy know she has developed real 'feelings' for him. You have heard women remark 'Why do all the good men turn out to be gay?' This situation can possibly be prevented if at the beginning of the relationship the woman can deal with the fact her friend is gay and to respect that reality."

Another potential minefield is when a woman becomes sexually attracted to a gay man and sets out to "convert" him into falling in love with her.

"Even this special situation can be mutually enjoyable if it involves a gay man who has labeled himself as 'bisexual' when in fact he does not want to admit his true homosexuality," Lensman says.

"Social acceptance means a lot to everyone, and sometimes this label seems more accepted than its 'gay' counterpart."

Ultimately, how does having his very own fag-hag make a gay man feel?

"Wonderful!" Lensman says "Women make the best friends for a gay male . . . I do not feel threatened at all to be involved in a social relationship with a 'fag-hag.' You just don't know how important it is to have a woman to talk to and be able to share everything with. It just isn't the same opening up to another guy about any insecurities or worries. Women make the best gossip partners imaginable."

Still in Question

A Sampling of Sex- and Sexual Orientation–Related Questions
Seeking Answers at Y? (www.yforum.com)

"I was watching some gay porn the other day and a lot of the anal sex just looked so uncomfortable. Are there any gay men who find anal sex uncomfortable and not really a turn-on?"

—LISA, 19, straight female

"I have heard that Asian women have smaller and tighter vaginas than women of other races. Is this true?"

—NATASHA, 21, female

"Are straight women as disgusted by lesbians as straight men are by gay men?"

—JASON, 27, white male, Baptist

"I would have to say that a lot of black women are sexy. But why do they claim to be 'freaks' in bed?"

—A.

"If man is supposed to be a higher animal, why do homosexuals engage in an activity, such as homosexual intercourse, that even animals do not practice?"

—CARYN, 38, white female, Christian

"I'm a heterosexual woman serving as best man at a same-sex (male) wedding. Should I throw a bachelor party, and if so, how should I go about it?"

—ANNA R., 26, straight female, Taoist

"Does a man with small hands, feet, nose, ears, etc. usually have a smaller-than-average penis?"

—LARRY K., 55, white

"My youngest daughter has told me she is bisexual. I have no problem with this because I love her very much and she is quite an intelligent young woman who knows her own power. But what exactly does 'bisexual' mean?"

—CHARLETTE H., female, Wiccan

NINE

On the Job:

Work

"**W**hile our family was watching a male ballet dancer, we wondered: Why do male ballet dancers augment their groin area with padding or a disproportionately large cup?"

—MIKE, 51, straight white male

Readers Respond

"Male dancers do not wear cups. To do so would hurt and restrict movement. What they do wear under their tights is sort of like a jock with one strap. It is very tight-fitting, in order to keep things in place, as when the dancer is in motion, and when he stops, so does everything else."

—REX T.

"A number of years ago I worked as a costumer for a top-rated ballet company. Male dancers take risks much like an athlete when dancing. Many of the maneuvers, including splits, jumps and bends, are potentially harmful to their genitals. In order to protect themselves, many dancers use a method of tucking themselves that would be difficult to explain. It gives added protection to the groin area. Also, keep in mind that the tights worn by dancers are very snug-fitting and have a tendency to accentuate all areas of the body."

—K. TAYLOR

"I danced with the New York City Ballet for nine years and with many of the biggest names in the business. I can assure you no one is augmenting themselves in any way. If anyone in our dressing room did, we would have laughed him out the door."

—CHARLES A., straight white male dancer

Y? Check

Edward MacDaniel, vice president of West New York, New Jersey–based Bal Togs, a major player in the ballet menswear industry, has a message for anyone spreading rumors that male ballet dancers augment themselves: Put a sock in it.

"Because for years dancers were thought of as effeminate or gay, some people think they are trying to put 'it' in your face, as if to say 'This is who we are' and prove their masculinity or manhood," he says. "That's a myth."

Bal Togs makes and sells thousands of "dance belts" for male ballet dancers monthly, most of which have a pouch in front and anywhere from a two- to four-inch elastic band that goes around the waist to act as support for the back for when a male dancer lifts a female.

And whence the bulge?

"To be quite blunt, you're pulling your balls up and putting it all in that pouch," he says. "You're putting the whole package together and pulling it up. Everything goes up instead of being allowed to be free. You have the tights that come up to the crotch, so there's no place to go but up, and it's compacted and tight."

In fact, the dance belt, which looks similar to a thong and works much like a jock strap, isn't really what causes the dancer to wind up with his best, ahem, foot, forward. It's what goes over the belt—the stretch-fabric "second skin" tights—that actually accentuates the area—as well as the muscular nature of male dancers in general.

"It's like wearing a Speedo (swimsuit) a size or two too small," MacDaniel says. "I'm not saying no one has *ever* put a sock in there, I guess, but you certainly don't have to do that to get that look."

? ? ?

"To medical professionals: What goes through your mind when you see a terrible trauma or a patient suffering from a particularly gory illness?"

—JENNIFER R., 30, black female

Readers Respond

"I'm a volunteer firefighter/EMT and have seen traumas and burn victims. It's not pretty, but when I'm on a call, I know that what I do helps my patient feel better. Any bit of reassurance I can give them, like a smile, might just help them know it is going to be OK. It is 'good acting' sometimes, but you just suck it up and do the job. And just ask any EMT, paramedic or firefighter: If something bothers us, we talk about it once we get back to our station. It's like therapy with people who saw the same things you did. In the field it's all professional, but at the station, you can talk it up."

—JOSIE, 22, white female, firefighter/EMT

"I'm a general internist, so I don't see a lot of gore, but I do get exposed to things that bother me, such as infected sebaceous cysts and fecal impactions (smells are what get to me). But someone's got to do it. Plus, the patients are often embarrassed about the problem, and I don't want to make them feel worse."

—S.G., 46, white female, physician

"My first thought: 'Yuck, gross and ick!' My immediate second thought: concern for the patient's welfare. While it may be yucky for me to see it, I'm not the one having to experience it. So my primary thoughts are concern for the individual. I don't hide that something is gross. The patient knows it is, I know it is and we're all more comfortable when that is openly acknowledged and discussed."

—LESLIE, 26, white female

"The only thing I can never get over is losing a patient, especially someone I grew fond of."

—DIANA, 53, Italian female, nurse

"I have worked as a firefighter/EMT for more than 10 years, and I've seen it all. The sight of burned flesh does not bother me. It looks waxy, like a candle. The smell, however, stays in your sinuses for weeks. What keeps you from being 'grossed out' is your professionalism. Would you return to a doctor who told you the infection you had was repulsive-looking and smelling? I think not. Most in this type of work have true compassion for their patients. If you don't, you will burn out. The worst things I see? Abused and neglected elderly and children. That makes me sick."

—KEVIN L., 29, white male, firefighter/EMT

Y? Check

People have a remarkable capacity to become desensitized—perhaps even indifferent—to grotesque things over time, says Frank Huyler, faculty member at the University of New Mexico Hospital and long-time emergency room doctor there.

What not all can do, however, is make snap decisions and maintain composure under pressure.

"Being a witness to an event and being partly responsible for its outcome are two different things," says Huyler, who wrote *The Blood of Strangers: Stories from Emergency Medicine* (Henry Holt, 2000). "If you miss a diagnosis or make a mistake or contribute to someone's demise, that is extremely difficult."

Those in emergency medicine don't forget about the disgusting and even nauseating things they've seen, he says, but the bottom line is they do become inured to distressing sights and events, so much so that it may take something remarkable to even register an impact.

"Just a couple weeks ago, a guy shot himself in the head and was brought into the ER alive and still breathing," Huyler says. "He had a big hole on one side of the head, and a big hole on the other. What was shocking . . . what really got to me was that when we were trying to help him breathe, we were squeezing in the air through the face mask, and with every squeeze, air was squirting out of both of the holes. It was horrible. I'd never seen anything like it."

Doctors and EMTs often use dark—what some might call insensitive—humor among each other to get beyond such images, although most don't spend a lot of time agonizing or "getting melodramatic" with each other to process the events of the day.

The overwhelming majority of the time, what sticks in their minds is those screwups, Huyler says.

"It's not so much about being shocked as it is about being very aware of the stakes. It's very humbling to realize how powerless you actually are most of the time. Most people get better no matter what you do, others will get worse no matter what you do, and some you can help. It does make you think about the larger questions."

? ? ?

"I have always wondered how a girl arrives at the point of displaying her private parts to strangers for money. Little girls aspire to be doctors, actresses and lawyers, but surely not nude dancers. At what point does money become more important than maintaining one's sexual privacy?"

—NOAH, male

Readers Respond

"As long as there are ignorant, sexually deprived losers, there will be strippers to take advantage of them."

—M. POWELL

"I started dancing when I was 19, for the money. My boyfriend's sister-in-law did and always had money to buy anything she wanted or go anywhere she wanted. I wanted this financial freedom as well. I was raised in a good family and have no body or sex issues. I now have a savings plan to cover the costs of university to study forensic science. Growing up, I was never taught that the body is something to be ashamed of. I believe I was blessed with a nice shape and pretty face for a reason. I might as well profit from it as much as I can while I've still got it."

—DIAMOND, 21, black/white female

"The real reason stems from the fact that I was molested many times as a child and raped many times as a young adult. I believe people like me strip to try to gain a sense of power and control over their sexuality. It is also a temporary rush and a high—a way to gain a false sense of self-esteem. Eventually this backfires. Perhaps there are people who work in the sex industry who don't have issues like this, and perhaps the occupation will not affect them adversely, but I have a hard time believing it."

—HEATHER, 22, white female

"I started stripping a month after high school. I kept the job for nine months. I'd begun to have sexual issues with it. I wasn't sexually abused as a child, but the sex-filled environment of strip clubs wore me down. I think it can be very damaging to attach a price to sexual favors."

—S.R., 22, white female

"I have dated or been involved with more than 150 strippers from New York, Atlanta and Miami over the past 24 years. Of them, 75 percent are on dope, 50 percent are into prostitution and dope, and 10 percent are my friends and have graduated college and gone on to better things. Most have been sexually or mentally abused, and it doesn't matter what type of family they come from. Many have Narcissistic Personality Disorder. Most are immature little girls looking for Daddy."

—JOEL, 42, white male

Y?Check

Many men would like to believe that female strippers are either stupid or morally inferior, says Carol Rambo, an associate professor of sociology at the University of Memphis known nationally for her research into the psychology of exotic dancing.

But what's really going on, according to her studies of male and female strippers and from personal experience as a stripper at a young age, is primarily a reaction to sexual abuse or betrayal experienced in early life.

Although money does play a role—dancers she has surveyed often discuss the need to support their children or pay for school—it is mostly a secondary factor, something strippers discuss as their primary motivation when generally it is not, says Rambo, who's studied stripping and childhood sexual abuse for nearly twenty years.

"The culture tells them, I'm supposed to be a good girl, but before I had a chance to be a good girl, dear old daddy or uncle or coach got me. You never got to be a good girl, so you disengage and disinvest . . . it's like, 'Fuck it, I can't get the rewards for following the rules anyway, so I might as well go this other route.' "

Researchers have found that in many cases, women react to abuse by becoming fearful of all things sexual, even purposely wearing oversize clothes. In other cases, says Rambo, who is an incest survivor herself, a girl might respond by becoming counterphobic—putting herself in the "line of fire" over and over again to try to master the trauma.

"So you see the little girl in a skintight outfit going to school. You say 'that little whore or slut,' but what we have here are people trying to work out their problems the best way they can . . . to come down on them with all this judgment and stigma makes it hard. So you wear your tight dress and say 'Fuck you, I'm going to get the best reward out of this that I can.' "

With male dancers, most don't claim to be sexually abused, but when pressed will often bring up tales of sexual exploits at young ages that if experienced by girls would be deemed abuse, Rambo says.

"I had one dancer tell me he was 7 the first time he had sex. His baby-sitter got hold of him, and she was 24. Yet he doesn't think of it as sexual abuse. He thinks he was lucky."

? ? ?

"**Do** people really believe that government employees are lazy, dumb and/or rude, or is this just a media stereotype that gets perpetuated?"

—JANET E., 50, trainer

Readers Respond

"I have yet to visit the DMV, post office, etc. without dealing with rude, obnoxious, unpleasant and unhelpful staff. I've been in other countries and government employees are very helpful and friendly, so it seems to be a U.S. thing."

—JAY, white female

"I'm a school teacher and my father was a postal worker. There is a grain of truth to the stereotypes. Most civil service jobs require a test. Jobs like teachers require a college degree and license. If you get the highest score, you get the job. You cannot be fired easily. This is supposed to ensure you got the job because you're qualified, not because of your uncle's influence. Strong job security makes sure you can do your job without being influenced by others. Does this system protect boneheads who are lazy and incompetent? Yes. Most government workers strive to do a good job, but you know the saying about one bad apple."

—STEVE, 28, black male, teacher

"I was a civil service employee for 15 years. Unfortunately, there are a number of employees who call in sick every Monday and Friday, do substandard work, file grievances at the smallest inconvenience and are verbally abusive to everyone they come in contact with. Those knotheads are the reason the stereotype you mention is alive and well."

—ALMA, 48, white female, educator

"My sister is an undersecretary to the Department of Something in Washington, D.C. I have heard her stories. It isn't that government employees are lazy, it's just that whole departments have no competition and no profit motive and, therefore, no reason to be efficient."

—STEVE, 45, white male

"It's the lazy, dumb and rude public that makes government workers respond the way they do."

—BRIAN, 26, white male, journalist

"Having spent three years working in a county hospital and three working for municipal government, I can't say government employees are lazy, dumb or rude. However, I did see a lot of sadness, boredom and people who made career choices based on security rather than interest or talent."

—MARY, 40, white female

"As an employee of a state academic institution related to health care, I find there is a culture of service here. None of us is a perfect little worker bee, but deep down we are motivated by this feeling. We work very hard to fulfill a need that is not always supported by the wealthier segments of society. The sad thing is that after a while, service people feel underappreciated and move on to other professions that might pay more or are less thankless, but aren't in service to anyone."

—JIM, 36, poet

Y? Check

A 2002 survey showed bad news about Americans' perceptions of the government work force. The 2,200 people questioned for a study by the Brookings Institution estimated that, on average, 48 percent of federal employees weren't doing their jobs well. Those same people thought 42 percent of private-sector employees were flops, as were 38 percent of people working for charities.

Although the negatives for every group were higher than expected, the results suggested government workers have an image problem.

But you'd get a different view if you asked government workers about their performance or how they feel about their jobs. Brookings did that, too, and found that in 2002, federal workers estimated 22 percent of their coworkers weren't doing their jobs well. That's just a little less than the amount of deadwood that people in the private sector estimated they had in their own workplaces.

Federal employees were also more upbeat about their jobs than a lot of Americans. There was widespread belief they were accomplishing something significant at work, and they were somewhat satisfied with their pay and benefits.

And although almost half of private-sector employees in the survey said they did their own jobs just for the paycheck, fewer federal employees said the same thing.

? ? ?

"Can waiters and waitresses give us diners some clues as to proper tipping?"

—H.

Readers Respond

"I was a waitress and bartender for eight years during college and my young party years. First, 15 percent is the standard tip for standard service. That number is derived from the total bill (which includes tax). If I get extraordinary service, I tip 20 percent. There will be those who say that you should not tip at all for bad service, but I disagree. I've had to work on nights when normal employees (day people) would have called in sick. Servers don't get sick pay or grievance time off, so take it easy on someone who could be having a bad day."

—DANIELLE C., 28

"Once, on a very busy night, when two other waitresses called in sick, I was running around, going crazy, and I wasn't able to give each customer the service I would have liked, and a couple let me know it. They were in their mid- to late twenties, and instead of a normal tip, they poured the salt on the table to spell 'you suck' and left a penny as a tip. Some people think the world revolves around them and don't take into consideration how hard other people have to work to keep them happy."

—J.R., 24, server

"While the previous example of the obnoxious table-salt note is an example of some pretty nasty people, the waitress who responded noted that she was overworked and couldn't provide adequate customer service. In that situation I would probably leave 5 percent, figuring that if she were working that many tables, the net result would be the same. Is she working harder? Absolutely. But that should be between her and management. If they're stretching her too thin, it's not in my nature to leave a 'normal' tip out of charity. That simply encourages the restaurant to not improve."

—TOM Y.

Y? Check

The appropriate restaurant tip for good service in the United States is currently 15 percent (as much as 20 percent for superior service), but it's by no means required—it should be earned, says Paul Paz, past president of the National Waiters Association and author of *Service at Its Best: A Guide to Becoming a Successful Server* (Prentice-Hall, 2001).

"It's a commission for services rendered, to ensure prompt service," says Paz, who's been a server for twenty-three years and is also a national consultant to the hospitality industry.

Leaving a below-average tip, or stiffing a server altogether, should be done only after carefully considering all the circumstances that led to poor service, he says. In addition, patrons should think about what they are trying to accomplish by leaving a lousy gratuity.

"If you're getting more attitude than service, without a doubt you can give a lower tip. But sometimes, the oven's broke, or someone didn't show up for work, or the place got busy very fast, and that's out of the server's control," Paz says.

If it appears that poor service or food was a result of restaurant management, then show your dissatisfaction not only by short-tipping, but by refusing to pay part of your overall bill, he says.

"If the customer is unhappy and simply leaves no tip, then there are no repercussions for management. If I'm the manager and decide to go with a 'short floor,' and because of that, my staff is completely overloaded, who's accountable? The waiter? No! It's the people running the joint."

Paz points out that old myths about certain races or types of people tipping worse than others are just that. In his presentations to the hospitality industry, he likes to show his list of the best and worst tippers.

The worst: alcohol drinkers, celebrities, church people, foreigners, journalists, minorities, New Yorkers, ravers, and vegetarians, among others.

The best: alcohol drinkers, celebrities, church people, foreigners, journalists, minorities, New Yorkers, ravers, and vegetarians, among others.

His point, he says, is that it's impossible to profile a "good" or "bad" tipper, because they come in all shapes, colors, and wallet sizes. Everything, he says, hinges on the service from the waiter.

"It boils down to being nice to people, knowing your craft and enjoying serving others," he says.

? ? ?

"**T**O actors and actresses: Is it possible to play a role in which you are falling in love with another person, and not have that affect you emotionally? I know it is a job, but the kisses that can curl the toes of audiences must surely curl your toes, as you are an actual participant."

—R.V., male

Readers Respond

"I'm an actor who studied under Lee Strasberg for four years. It surely is possible to play a steamy love scene and not fall in love. In fact, you could very much dislike the other actor and still pull off a steamy scene. Actors trained by Strasberg use a technique called 'substitution,' whereby through our senses we create someone in our personal lives and imbue that person upon the actor we are playing the scene with. After we're done, we can get up and walk away from it and, though emotionally involved as it may be, we know we 'created' it and it's not reality."

—M.P.

"I've been an actor for more than 20 years. The kisses can be nice at the start, but remember, at least in stage acting, the makeup may not look all that great up close. It is a shallow thrill, and after the 100th performance the thrill is bound to wear off. It really is just make-believe."

—MARTY K., 42, white male

Y? Check

Actors do, after all, act, says Arlene Schulman, who has been everything from actor to director to acting coach for more than twenty years in the New York City and New Jersey areas.

"It is a common misconception that actors 'become' their characters and that they actually get lost in the feelings and experiences they have. In fact, actors work at learning how to access their own emotions and experiences and use them to live truthfully in imaginary circumstances," says Schulman, an associate member of the Society of Stage Directors and Choreographers and associate director at New Jersey Repertory Company.

An actor "in the moment" can feel the emotion, but that doesn't mean feeling love for the person playing opposite them, she says.

"For professional actors, this is a job that they do over and over all their lives. They could hardly become emotionally involved with everyone they work with," Schulman says. " 'Falling in love' with another character doesn't mean that you, the actor, will necessarily even like the other actor. That's why they call it acting."

There can lie a danger in that actors are often by their nature sensitive people whose emotions are close to the surface, Schulman notes.

"Working intensely in close contact with other actors for extended periods can enhance any natural attraction you may feel, and because you are actively using those emotions that in everyday life and with ordinary people might be suppressed or much more slowly awakened, relationships can fire up quickly," she says. "These usually cool down just as quickly when the show is over. And they have nothing to do with deep and real love. They are purely about physical chemistry and emotional vulnerability."

Still in Question
A Sampling of Work-Related Questions
Seeking Answers at Y? (www.yforum.com)

"Can anyone in the fashion industry tell me why the runway models have such outrageous clothes that nobody would be caught dead in?"

—R.J.

"I am a white, 43-year-old female who has taught preschool for about 20 years. Why is the occupation of teaching young children so low-paying?"

—CIL, 43, white female

"Why do farmers always seem to leave one large tree in the middle of their plowed fields?"

—A. SANDERSON

"Do most women find men in the military attractive, especially when in their fatigues?"

—AIRMAN H., 19, white male, U.S. Air Force

"Does having acne make an individual less likely to be selected for a job or professional career?"

—MARY A.

"Why does a principal or school official have the right to search students, but the police need to have a warrant to search someone?"

—SARA S., 17

Getting in on the Conversation

Over the years of this project, I've often asked myself—particularly late at night, pounding away at my keyboard in my tiny garage office after a long day at work—*Why, exactly, did I start Y?*

Each time I take a crack at an answer, I usually find myself going back in time to the holiday trips my family took in our '72 Kingswood Estate station wagon.

Back then, every Thanksgiving, Christmas, and Easter we embarked on an interminably long drive to see our relatives. (All right, so it was only two hours from Glen Ellyn, Illinois, to Milwaukee, but as a kid it seemed like forever.)

I had four extremely bright, articulate older brothers, Dean, Paul, Mark, and Steve. No matter how hard I tried, they never failed to come off as smarter than me. Steve and I, being the youngest, always found ourselves dispatched to the far, chilly reaches of the back of the station wagon, where we lay during the journey, listening to our older brothers discuss, fight about, solve, then fight more about the small and large topics of the day.

Although Steve, being quite up on things for a just-barely teen, could occasionally insert himself into these marathon talkfests, I found myself for the most part listening in a cold-cocked state of awe.

How can I make them see that I give a damn, too? I wondered.

What I learned unconsciously then about what makes give-and-take work with others is dramatically similar to what I found has worked during the past decade, while I've moderated thousands of cross-cultural exchanges at Y?, recruited and conversed with minorities in the newspaper industry, and given workshops about diversity dialogue to business executives, nonprofit volunteers, government workers, and college students.

If you really want to add your two cents' worth or get someone else to add theirs, especially in conversations with folks who might intimidate you, try the following:

- **Get to know more about yourself first.** What's motivating you? Why do you want to engage someone in the first place? Is it for the right reasons? The answers might surprise you and help you figure out how best to approach someone. A good friend once told me the real reason I started Y? wasn't because I wanted to learn more about "Buddhists in Asia or lesbians in San Francisco," but because I wanted to learn something more about myself. He was right. Acknowledging that has helped give me perspective when encountering someone different from myself.

- **Pick your spots.** Wait for a real opening; don't create a fake one. It's during those down times between all the "vital" conversation that we can most easily find a direct path to someone's point of view. If you spend enough time sitting in the cubicle next to someone of a different culture, chances are there will come a time—over food, perhaps, during a power outage, celebrating the company's decision to pare your health benefits again instead of imposing layoffs—when the topic you've been dying to broach will wend its way naturally into the discussion.

- **Keep it simple, at first.** Some of the best questions I've gotten at Y?, those that prompted the most telling replies, were easy to digest, such as "When did you know you were gay?" I think I got twenty-five great replies the first day I put that one up on the site. Once you've made some inroads with someone and gained their trust, you can progress to the "Doesn't it hurt when you do it in that position?" types of inquiries. Baby steps!

- **Don't pull your punches.** No one appreciates feigned interest or secondary motives. We're all big kids. It's all in the delivery. I'll take an earnest "Why do all you white folks pick your noses?" over some psycho-babble or moral statement any day. It's what comes from the heart that counts most—and captures people's interest.

- **Keep assumptions at bay.** Don't pepper your questions or comments with preconceived notions. Have an open mind. Remember, you're trying to gain something from the discussion, not prove a point. No one learns anything being a know-it-all or by talking with one.

- **Expect the unexpected.** Never assume you've heard it all. You're much less likely to get offended that way. And besides, righteous indignation never helped anyone pocket even the tiniest gem of wisdom. Even after moderating thousands of questions sent in to Y?, I admit I can still get thrown for a loop, at least temporarily, with some submissions. But after discovering that questions about white people smelling like wet dogs and Arabs wiping themselves with their bare hands aren't completely without merit, I'm much less inclined to be taken aback.

So there you have it. My quick guide on how to enter the arena of cross-cultural dialogue without getting a punch in the gut. But it still leaves me back where I started, with my first question: Why did I do all this?

Ultimately, I believe I did it in a quest to prove to myself and others that, despite our self-doubts, ignorance, or even apathy, there is still a part of us that wants to *know* and wants others to *see* that we want to know. Despite the worst parts of our nature, the bigotry, bias, and baiting, we are inclined, perhaps even programmed, to rise above those faults to show others that we do give a damn.

Somehow, instinctively, I found my place in that '72 station wagon: to play the part of the inquisitor. I sensed that the best I could hope for, the surest way for me to convince my family that I had a decent head on my shoulders, that I cared about something and wasn't some unfeeling, unknowing piece of driftwood, was for them to discover that I wanted, deep down, to know something more than I already knew. Or at least thought I knew.

In that tiny world, among all that charged intellect and opinion, I had only one shot. So I took it.

I asked. And asked some more. And you know what? They answered. And before I knew it, I was in on the conversation.

—P.J.M.

More Questions?

Dare to ask or answer a question that goes straight to the core of our differences. Learn how we're similar in ways you never imagined. If you have something to add to the dialogue at Y? or for a future volume of *I Can't Believe You Asked That!,* please send it to:

Y Forum
P.O. Box 8071
Fleming Island, FL 32006
yforum@yforum.com

Or visit www.yforum.com

We'll be sure to credit you for your contribution, either with your full name, initials, or pseudonym—depending on your preference and whether you feel your submission is too daring! Thank you.

SPEECHES AND KEYNOTE ADDRESSES:
Y? director Phillip J. Milano is an in-demand speaker available for lectures and presentations related to diversity communication and the phenomenon of the Y? project. He can be contacted at the above address.

About the Author

Phillip J. Milano is director and editor-in-chief of Y? The National Forum on People's Differences (www.yforum.com). He is an eighteen-year newspaper veteran and an editor for *The Florida Times-Union* in Jacksonville. He is past chairman of the Recruitment and Youth Development Committee of The Newspaper Association of America's Diversity Board, as well as a featured speaker at diversity-related seminars and college programs. Mr. Milano's articles on diversity and recruitment have appeared in *Presstime* and *The American Editor.* He is also founder of The National Diversity Newspaper Job Bank (www.newsjobs.com), regarded as the nation's premier newspaper recruiting website for minorities and women. Mr. Milano received his master's of business administration from Northern Illinois University and his bachelor's of science in journalism from Southern Illinois University. He lives with his wife, Robin, and three sons in Florida.